GOVERNMENT MEDIA
Autonomy and After

About the Editor

G. S. Bhargava is a veteran journalist whose last assignment was as resident editor of the Indian Express at Hyderabad and other Andhra Pradesh centres. As Principal Information Officer to the Government of India (1978-80) and earlier as a frequent participant in radio and television programmes, he has been keenly interested in the working of the electronic media in India and the need for their autonomy.

GOVERNMENT MEDIA
Autonomy and After

Edited by
G.S. Bhargava

Published for

Institute of Social Sciences
By
CONCEPT PUBLISHING COMPANY PVT. LTD,
NEW DELHI-110059

ISBN : 978-81-7022-366-5

Edition 2019

Published and Printed by

Concept
Since 1974

Concept Publishing Company Pvt. Ltd.
A/15-16, Commercial Block, Mohan Garden,
New Delhi-110059 (INDIA)
T : +91 11 25351460, +91 11 25351794
E : publishing@conceptpub.com, *W* : www.conceptpub.com

Cataloging in Publication Data--Courtesy: D.K. Agencies (P) Ltd. <docinfo@dkagencies.com>

Seminar on "Autonomy and After: Government Media" (1990 : New Delhi, India)
Government media : autonomy and after / edited by G.S. Bhargava.
pages cm
Reprint. Originally published: 1991.
"... Institute of Social Sciences is organising a Seminar on "Autonomy and After: Government Media" on 28 April, 1990"--Page ix.
Includes bibliographical references and index.
ISBN 9788170223665

1. Broadcasting policy--India--Congresses. 2. Public broadcasting--India--Congresses. I. Bhargava, G. S., 1925- editor. II. Institute of Social Sciences (New Delhi, India), organizer. III. Title.

LCC HE8689.9.I4S46 1990 | DDC 384.50954 23

Preface

THE enactment of the Prasar Bharati Act in 1990 did not end the topicality and relevance of autonomy for the electronic media from direct government control. The subject remains on the agenda of intellectual fora, political thinkers and concerned professionals and individual citizens. The Chanda Committee of 1976, the Verghese Committee of 1977, the Prasar Bharati Bill of 1979 and the most recent intervention, the Prasar Bharati Bill as ultimately adopted by Parliament highlighted the evils of control of information and electronic media and the need for a creative atmosphere for their proper functioning as an input in national development. But the law on the statute book has fallen short of expectations.

This book has emerged from the proceedings of a seminar organised by the Institute of Social Sciences on "Autonomy and After: Government Media" on 28 April 1990 at the Parliament House Annexe. The Bill was in the consideration stage then.

In the midst of seminars, talks and conferences galore on this topic since the introduction of the Prasar Bharati Bill in Parliament we organised this seminar to focus the attention on "what after autonomy". What are the difficulties, as well as necessary organisational, financial and technical prerequisites that would impede or aid the actual functioning of autonomy on the ground. The presentations were wide ranging and from varying perspectives and vantage points: administrative, technical, academic and journalistic. Conceptual as well as constitutional aspects of media autonomy also came up for discussion.

We hope this collection of papers can serve as a modest though important input in this long but vital on-going struggle for autonomy for the electronic media as a first steadfast step towards their independence ultimately.

Mr G S Bhargava planned and co-ordinated this seminar; but for whom this publication would not have been possible. The Institute of Social Sciences is grateful to him. He was ably assisted by Dr Girish Kumar, Ms Priti Anand and Mr P N Kuttappan of the Institute.

New Delhi
March 9, 1991

George Mathew

Contributors

S R Bommai—President, Janata Dal; former Chief Minister of Karnataka.

B S S Rao—Director (Information), National Institute of Rural Development, Hyderabad.

Ramaswamy R Iyer—Member, Public Enterprises Selection Board, New Delhi.

H K Paranjape—Eminent economist, columnist and editor of *Janata*, Bombay.

P C Chatterji—Formerly Director-General of Akashvani and Doordarshan.

Harish Khanna—Former Director-General, Doordarshan and now Executive Director, Family Planning Foundation.

K K Sud—Director, Research & Publication Centre, Media Foundation of the Non-Aligned, New Delhi; formerly Chief of the All India Radio News Bureau.

Harsaran Pandey—Producer of Doordarshan current affairs programmes for 14 years; presently public relations officer of UNICEF.

O P Khushu—Director, Technical Centre, Asia-Pacific Broadcasting Union, Kuala Lumpur; formerly Engineer-in-Chief, Doordarshan.

B N Koul—Director, Distance Education, Indira Gandhi National Open University, New Delhi.

Contents

I am happy to learn that the Institute of Social Sciences is organising a Seminar on "Autonomy and After: Government Media" on 28 April, 1990.

Right to information is an invaluable asset of any democratic system. In this age of information explosion, command over information is an unmistakable index of power. The people of India, being the real source of authority, must naturally have free access to all sources of information and to the media responsible for its proper dissemination to make our democracy more vibrant.

Electronic media with their all-pervading ambit have, of late, become the symbols of cultural continuity and change. By championing the causes of education, information and entertainment, these media have become agencies of socialisation and knowledge transmission. The relationship between the State and the electronic media has, therefore, become a subject of interesting public debate. I am sure that the discussions in the Seminar, which is being organised at a very opportune time, would throw some illuminating beams on the question of autonomy of our electronic media in the context of our cultural configuration. The on-going dialogue would not only sharpen the contours of our understanding but would also come up with practical solutions for arriving at a national consensus on this vital issue.

I wish the Seminar all success.

New Delhi
April 19, 1990

Rabi Ray
Speaker, Lok Sabha

Inaugural Address

S R Bommai

FIRST of all, let me congratulate the Institute of Social Sciences for organising this seminar on Autonomy and After: Government Media.

It was in 1977 that autonomy for the government-owned electronic media, meaning All India Radio and Doordarshan became an issue in the general election. Until then it was a desirable objective which Pandit Nehru had envisaged for realisation in the unspecified future. The failure of the Indira Gandhi government to act on the recommendations of the Chanda Committee, set up in 1966, and the blatant misuse of the media during the emergency, for personal and party propaganda had lent urgency to the issue.

The Janata Government set up a working group under the chairmanship of Shri B G Verghese to prepare the ground—so to say—for the promised autonomy for the media. The Verghese Committee had made a thorough study of the subject in the national and international perspectives and suggested a blue print for the contemplated change. The Prasar Bharati Bill of 1979 was based on those proposals, although it deviated in some vital respects from them. The Bill had been referred to a joint select committee of the two Houses of Parliament but before the task had been accomplished the Lok Sabha was dissolved and the legislation lapsed.

The National Front government has taken up the thread and has introduced in the Lok Sabha in December last the present Prasar Bharati Bill. Although it is a vast improvement on the 1979 Bill, there is still widespread criticism that the autonomy it envisages is not adequate for the purpose of meaningful change in the structure and functioning of the media.

Basically, there is general agreement that the media should be autonomous, that is free of control by the Executive in its operation, and should develop the necessary ethos to fulfil its three-fold objective of informing, instructing and entertaining the community at large.

While introducing the Bill in the Lok Sabha, the Minister of Information and Broadcasting, Shri P Upendra, described it as "a charter of freedom to give choice to the people of India through the broadcast medium in the fulfilment of their fundamental freedom of speech and expression." In that context, he has said that the persons who direct and run the proposed corporation are more crucial than the structure of the organisation for making the autonomy meaningful.

So it is the task of all supporters of autonomy for the media to focus on conditions which will produce such persons and such a structure.

In this connection, I am glad that this seminar will not confine itself to the letter of the draft legislation but will go beyond to see what autonomy should mean both conceptually and institutionally. In other words, since an autonomous broadcast organisation cannot be a hot house growth but has to be evolved over time, it is necessary to have a long-term perspective. Conventions can be created. Structures can be modified and rebuilt—provided we are clear in our mind about the objective—which is a broadcast set up to articulate the urges and aspirations of our society, without fear or favour. I am happy to inaugurate the seminar and take this opportunity to wish its deliberations all success.

1

Introduction

THE idea of autonomy from direct Government control for All India Radio was first mooted in 1966 by a body of officials called the Chanda Committee. It recommended conversion of All India Radio into an autonomous corporation. All India Radio was the only electronic medium then and the merits and demerits of its continuance as a Government department were examined by the committee. Its conclusion was for "liberation" of Akashvani from "rigid financial and administrative procedures of Government" so that it could be "a creative medium in the Indian context." Until then the only authoritative pronouncement on the subject was an off-the-cuff remark by Nehru in the Constituent Assembly in 1948 that "my own view of the set-up for broadcasting is that we should approximate, as far as possible, to the British model, the BBC, that is to say, it would be better if we had a semi-autonomous corporation under the Government, of course, with the policy controlled by the Government, otherwise not conducted as a Government department."

What Nehru called "a semi-autonomous corporation" became the vogue for several Government institutions during the eighteen years which intervened the publication of the Chanda Committee report. Besides the Election Commission, the Union Public Service Commission and the office of the Comptroller and Auditor-General of India which are declared autonomous in the Constitution itself, others like the Reserve Bank of India, the Central Vigilance Commissioner and the Public Enterprises Selection Board have been put into that category. It is not clear whether the Chanda Committee examined in detail the magnitude and nature of the autonomy enjoyed by these institutions but, by and large, the impression was that the executive could not directly control their functioning. This was despite the Mundhra case in which Mr T T Krishnamachari as Union Finance Minister made the Reserve Bank Governor toe the line in investing heavily in the companies of Haridas Mundhra.

In other words, autonomous institutions had not then been drained of initiative and independence as most of them have been in recent years. Secondly, Ashok Chanda and his colleagues were prompted more by the positive need for developing All India Radio as "a creative medium in Indian conditions" than by the negative aspect of preventing or stopping the misuse of the medium. Ironically, Indira Gandhi's tenure as minister of information and broadcasting in the Government of Lal Bahadur Shastri was marked by high tolerance of debate and dissent in the current affairs programmes of All India Radio. She had also set up the Chanda Committee of her own volition without any prodding by the Opposition or the liberals in her party.

The next occasion when the demand for autonomy for the electronic media—Doordarshan had come into being then, even if gingerly—was during the 1977 elections to the Lok Sabha. It was largely as a reaction to the blatant and widespread misuse of the media during the 1975-77 emergency. Indira Gandhi who was so "liberal" as minister of information and broadcasting swung to the other extreme as prime minister. She buried the report of the Chanda Committee which she herself had set up in a previous incarnation. She openly questioned the need for credibility for the Government media. In the run up to and during the emergency, egged on by Sanjay Gandhi, she had ridden rough shod over the media. The Janata Government in 1977 set up a committee under Kuldip Nayar to catalogue instances of such misuse of the media.

Autonomy for the electronic media was an electoral commitment of the Janata Government. The contemplated autonomy had not, however, been spelt out in the party's election manifesto beyond indicating that it would mean freeing the radio and television of Government control. The Verghese Committee set up in 1977 had thus the dual task of providing for a situation in which the media could not be misused and developing the concept of autonomy positively. The positive content of the Verghese Committee report stands out more than its reaction to what had happened during the emergency although, unlike the Chanda Committee, it owed its establishment largely to the emergency experience.

Interestingly, although there was a proliferation of autonomous institutions in the first three decades of independence and a trend towards the erosion of their autonomy had started, the concept of autonomy had not fallen into disrepute then, as it has now. It was common for retired officials and other hangers-on of the establishment to find cosy berths in the administrative sections of professional organisations like the Indian Council of Agricultural Research or the National Council of Scientific Research. But the professionals by and large did not reduce themselves to be tools of the political masters. A chief election commissioner would do the bidding of the Government in conducting or not conducting an election or in allowing ballot rigging in support of the ruling party or one or more judges of the Supreme Court would favour the Government in their verdicts but science and research did not begin to subserve the glory of the ruling dynasty until the closing years of the 1980s.

But as I said earlier, the phenomenon did not figure in the Verghese Committee's report. It spread the canvas to look upon the media as an instrument of development and tool of enlarging individual and community freedom and recommended a structure for the proposed broadcasting corporation or Akash Bharati, as it was recommended to be christened, which would be practically independent of the Government—administratively, financially and even in policy matters.

To quote from the Verghese Committee report, "In the Indian situation the objective of communication policy must be to awaken the people, inform, mobilise and educate them to be democratic citizens. . , ensure equity and equality of opportunity, safeguard national values, preserve both unity and accepted national goals." The Janata Government's legislation on the subject, the Prasar Bharati Bill of 1979, fell far short of the Verghese Committee's approach. Nevertheless, subject to improvements, it would have converted the two media into a single corporation—with two wings—independent of departmental control and Government meddling in its day-to-day functioning. It would have above all provided a framework for autonomous operation of the media and, in the process, promoted the necessary professionalism. But before the Bill could be passed, the Janata Government was undermined by a section of its own members in whose calculations autonomy for the media weighed very little.

The next ten years were a virtual repetition of the earlier decade, except that there was no formal imposition of "an emergency." Values had come to be more thoroughly eroded and institutions systematically denuded of their content. Hypocrisy had become the order of the day. For instance, journalists and others who never tired of professing allegiance to independence and functional autonomy did not hesitate to work for the media irrespective of the content of their programmes. A new breed of experts who were all things to all men (defenders of the emergency in 1975, its critics in 1977, supporters of all that Indira Gandhi and her son did in the next ten years and then advisers of the Janata Dal dispensation) had come into being. In short, what is called the ethos conducive to the autonomous functioning of the media has not developed.

It is against this background that the 1989 version of the Prasar Bharati Bill, which Parliament has passed with major changes, is to be examined. It is an improvement on the 1979 version in some respects but a setback in others. For instance, among the objectives of the corporation or Prasar Bharati, the 1979 Bill included "giving adequate coverage to the composite culture of the country as well as sports and games, serving the rural, illiterate and weaker sections of the people, keeping in view the special needs of the youth, social and cultural minorities, the tribal communities and those residing in the border regions, backward or remote areas and upholding the secular ideal and promoting a spirit of truth and enquiry in the country among all sections of the people."

These were reduced to the following prosaic paragraph in the present law for reasons known only to its authors: "providing adequate coverage to the diverse cultures and languages of the various regions of the country by broadcasting appropriate programmes."

The concept of composite culture of India amidst the multiplicity of languages and different religions is worth inculcating in our people, and radio, and especially television, are the most effective means of doing it. There is also no reason why anyone should have taken umbrage at making it an objective of the proposed broadcasting corporation. (It is also a reflection on the aversion of some political parties to the concept of composite culture as distinct from diverse cultures. Despite the multiplicity of India's languages and the religious diversity of its people the Indian culture is composite).

At the structural level both the 1979 and the present law miss a basic point, that it will have to ensure competition within the framework of Government ownership of the media, competition between radio and television, competition between the national network and the regionally sponsored programmes. As establishing an additional television channel is said to cost not less than Rs. 2,000 crore, without taking into account the maintenance expenses, we will have to make do with the prevailing physical structure by having low-power transmitters and using them for transmitting regionally made programmes.

More importantly, the Verghese Committee recommendation that universities and other similar institutions should be allowed to establish franchise stations for transmitting their own programmes within a limited physical reach has been ignored. This would have ended the monopoly and monotony of the so-called national programmes and provide the viewer with a choice, even if limited in scope and duration. It is time this vast country of ours, with its rich diversity, is served by a diversified network of radio and television stations catering to the varied tastes of the people.

In short, the purpose of autonomy will not be served if Akashvani and Doordarshan contiaue their centralised functioning with the bulk of the programmes originating from Delhi or other cities. The proposal for a second TV channel to be controlled by the respective State Governments does not serve the purpose because the viewer or listener will in that case can only choose between what emanates from Delhi or a State capital. The programmes must have a local flavour to appeal to the people and be able to serve as sources of information and education.

In this context, certain "facts of life" have to be borne in mind while considering the development of the electronic media in our country. First and foremost, although television as the visual medium is more effective, radio is the only means of reaching the bulk our people in the villages and the far-flung border areas. This is because of the high cost of television sets, the indifferent management of community watching centres and the non-availability of electricity even in villages claimed to have been electrified. According to available statistics, there are about 2,25,00,000 or 22.5 million television sets—both black and white and colour—in the country as on December 31, 1989. This is undoubtedly a sizeable number but a drop in the ocean of our vast population. The number of community sets is put at about 38,000. With the craze for video viewing, most of the rich rural homes use their television sets for watching movies. Even small villages have video parlours and video lending has become big business.

The reach of the radio is put at about 95 per cent of the population and a little more than 83 per cent of the area of the country. Thanks to the transistor radio, non-availability of power is no hindrance to its operation. Cost-wise, too, it is well within the reach of most people including agricultural labourers. There are as many as 92 full-fledged radio stations in the country but not all of them are programme generators. If they are developed into such facilities and if there is a wider practice of exchange of programmes among them, the radio can be an alternative to television for those who cannot afford the latter.

Secondly, the way in which television has been developed in the country with the accent on hardware, the introduction of colour television and the mindless multiplication of transmitters, it is not possible to do away with commercial programmes. The estimated revenue from advertising of Doordarshan in 1989 was Rs. 19.5 crore. The cumulative effect of the neglect of programme content and switch-over to commercialiation is the growth of consumerism which is vitiating the outlook especially of the youth. There does not seem to be an escape from it in the short run. Over the years, however, the very surfeit of consumerism may put the viewers off as it has happened in the U.S.

Thirdly, as much as Government control of the media, paucity of professionalism among media practitioners is responsible for the potential of television not being realised in creative terms. Conversion of the media units into one or two autonomous corporations will not automatically solve this problem. It requires a long term and sustained effort to shift the emphasis to quality and promotion of professionalism. It is worth noting, in this context, that the government media draw heavily on journalists working with the newspapers owned mostly by private interests. It is more so for the current affairs programmes. And it is these non-employees of the media units who set the style for conformism and opportunism. Very few of them have the moral courage to refuse to participate in programmes which, they know, are meant to serve narrow political purposes. Against this background, it is too much to expect the employees of Doordarshan and Akashvani to be assertive towards the authorities.

Current affairs programmes on the radio, and more so on television, account for no more than 20 per cent of the broadcast time. Yet they receive most of the attention of the critics, not always deservedly. The news bulletins are often singled out for criticism. One can legitimately—and in fact should—take exception to propaganda in the name of news telecasts as it used to happen in Rajiv Gandhi's days and now under the Chandra Sekhar dispensation. It was not so under the National Front Government. Still, the quality of the news bulletins left much to be desired because of the skewed evaluation of news. Most newspapers are also guilty of it. We have hundreds of journalists concentrated in Delhi and other places to chase stories largely of political gossip and speculation. The villages come into focus only when there is a riot, a flood or a road or rail accident.

The two news agencies, despite the large bounty they enjoy from the Government, or perhaps because of it, do not venture out into new areas for news gathering. They concentrate on "events" to the neglect of "processes." The newspapers also do not have the incentive to break new ground, except with honourable exceptions. No wonder, therefore, the electronic media are afflicted by the stereotyped monotony of news presentation.

Against this background, autonomy for the electronic media would require imaginative action to break with the past and strive for conceptual clarity to link objectives to practicality. The Prasar Bharati Act, 1990, fails on this account, especially because the legislation has been further whittled down during the passage through Parliament.

In this context, the note presented by Vikram Sarabhai at a conference of the Society for International Development in New Delhi in November 1969 is extremely relevant (see Annexure). First and foremost, he cast the electronic media, especially television, in the role of "an initiator of change and development." Secondly, he rightly pointed out that development of software for the media to perform the task is more important and formidable than hardware development. There was a time in Rajiv Gandhi's regime when television transmitters were launched at the rate of almost one very day but they had nothing to transmit except Rajiv Gandhi's immature and half-baked "ideas" and the propaganda accompanying them. There was a similar experience in 1975 when the SITE experiment was launched taking advantage of an American provided satellite. Thirdly, there is "urgent need" to disseminate information to the people—information about fertilisers, seeds, scientific and other discoveries, goods and services, new living patterns, economic, political and other developments—"for the rapid and sustained growth" of the country. Fourthly, Sarabhai wanted the increasing use of the media "to enrich life in the isolated rural communities."

There is another important point made in the Sarabhai paper. It is that agencies responsible for individual fields such as information and broadcasting, education, agriculture, health, family planning, etc. should be able to "buy television time" for programmes related to the discharge of their respective responsibilities. For this purpose, he suggested the creation of a national authority "to regulate and manage the mass communication system without itself taking total responsibility for software." Ten years later, the Verghese Committee developed the concept further and provided the framework for socially purposeful media. Without such a conceptual framework, the law has been content with administrative changes.

To provide an opportunity for exchange of informed opinions on the concept and practice of media autonomy, the Institute of Social Sciences, New Delhi, held a seminar in New Delhi in April last. By that time, the plethora of seminars on the Prasar Bharati Bill, 1989, had ended and the Information and Broadcasting Ministry was said to be examining their conclusions and recommendations. In other words, the last word on the subject had been spoken. So the Information and Broadcasting Ministry officials invited to the seminar had no incentive to attend it. In fact, one of its key officials even questioned the need for a further conceptual discussion. Doordarshan officials to a man/woman stayed away, as if advised by the authorities not to share their thoughts with plebians. The only notable exception was Shri O P Khushu, Engineer-in-Chief, Doordarshan. The leaders of political parties including Shri L K Advani, Shri Vasant Sathe, Shri Vithal Gadgil, Shri Raj Mohan Gandhi, Shri Inderjit Gupta and others did not also give us the benefit of their wisdom. Still, the seminar attended by scholars, media practitioners, administrators and journalists covered plenty of new ground and yielded fresh ideas. This is the report of its deliberations, including the papers presented.

Meanwhile, while the newspapers generally went about belittling the prospect of the electronic media becoming autonomous, because the pictures of the then Prime Minister and the Information Minister appeared too often in the news bulletins or names of foreigners were mispronounced, the Government brought forward amendments to its draft legislation, some of which curtailed the contemplated autonomy.* The net result of this two-way exercise is that autonomy and accountability of the proposed broadcasting corporation are judged solely in terms of the authority which the Government would wield vis-a-vis the organisation. During the brief National Front Government period, although the media were under Government control, the contents of the current affairs programmes, including the news bulletins on the radio and television, improved in the direction of independence and professionalism. The most illustrative instance was during the then Prime Minister's press conference on July 20, 1990, when a Doordarshan correspondent asked a somewhat provocative question on Kashmir. Until then the practice for Government media personnel had been to record, almost mutely, ministerial pronouncements and present them as news. But it was a shortlived experience because after Chandra Sekhar became prime minister the old practice of the media propagating official platitudes was resumed with a vengeance.

The purpose of recalling the development is to stress the inadequate conceptual backing for the new Prasar Bharati Bill which was content with formal change of administrative control from the Government. Following the amendment of the bill before it was finally adopted by Parliament, the situation became worse with the provision for direct involvement by Parliament, meaning a few vocal MPs, in the day-to-day working of the media. In the words of Dr. Ramaswami R. Iyer, who has made an intensive study of the working of autonomous corporations, "it would appear that neither the Government nor Parliament was willing to repose any confidence or trust in the very high-level body which they were establishing." Experience shows that it is easier for professionals to overcome governmental interference and bureaucratic meddling than to survive direct involvement by MPs. For instance, when Mrs. Gandhi as Minister of Information and Broadcasting, allowed adequate latitude to media professionals in organising radio programmes, the

* See Annexure 3 for the law as amended.

MPs never missed an opportunity to snipe at independent-minded participants in the radio programmes.

It is not pleasant but has to be noted that Mr. P. Upendra as Mr. V.P. Singh's Minister of Information and Broadcasting, did not live up to his professions on media autonomy and was lacking in conceptual clarity on the subject. His claim of several seiminars and discussions on the draft bill having projected public thinking on the subject is denied first by the fact that most of the non-official professionals were critical of many of the provisions of the Bill. More importantly, the law as it ultimately emerged from Parliament was sharply different, in vital respects, from the draft legislation.

Similarly, the Government tendency to look upon media autonomy as a means of putting the radio and television in an adversarial position is shortsighted. Clauses 24 and 25 of the Act, added to the draft legislation, negate the very basis of "liberation from rigid. ... procedures of government" which was the crux of the Chanda Committee report as long ago as 1966. They provide for supersession of the board of directors of the proposed corporation—as in the case of a municipal corporation—with Parliament rubberstamping it. The contention that failure to comply with the Government's demand for "information" should be seriously dealt with by way of supersession of the board of governors reveals lack of understanding of the working of a media unit. Credibility will be the core of its existence. If, in the interest of credibility, the corporation will have to carry out Government directions under protest, it should be welcomed. The bill as originally drafted is adequate for ensuring the issuance of directions and their compliance.

It seems, unfortunately, that officials and MPs still think in terms of managing the media with threats of dismissal of functionaries and supersession of management boards. No eminent person worth his or her name will allow himself or herself to be subjected to such humiliation.

As Shri Ramaswamy Iyer's paper presented to the seminar shows, the autonomy enjoyed in practice by most of the autonomous corporations is far from absolute or even total. It is hedged in by so many practical limitations. That was why the tenure of the board of directors of the proposed corporation is sought to be entrenched. The demand for a fool-proof system for their selection is also meant to reduce the possibility of the corporation being loaded with persons beholden to the Government.

Finally, accountability to Parliament does not mean that the corporation should be made to accommodate the whims and fancies of members of Parliament, individually or collectively. For instance, there was too much fuss about the screening of a television serial on Tipu Sultan as if the Ramayana and Mahabharata are historically authentic! Why should not episodes from history be fictionalised without narrow-minded persons weighing them in religious scales? Why should not Doordarshan be allowed to project diverse aspects of historical and other events and issues? Being a highly visible medium, television is more accountable to the people than Parliament members or the occupants of the treasury benches. Its performance should be judged by its peers represented by the broadcasting council which should be strengthened as a watchdog body and constituted on the lines of the Press Council of India.

No doubt, the National Front Government was helpless in the matter as it needed the support of the Congress-I for the passage of the legislation. The Communists also were lukewarm towards the idea of autonomous Government media, notwithstanding the march of *glasnost* in Gorbachov's Soviet Union where the media have become unprecedentedly autonomous. The BJP., despite Mr L K Advani being its leader, did not show much interest in the matter. The Ramajanmabhoomi was more important for it. In spite of all these negative factors, the legislation could have been spared its ultimate distortion if the concerned minister had a mind of his own and had not been too dependent on bureaucrats.

It seems in retrospect that efforts to vest autonomy in Government media in India are star-crossed. Mr. Advani's 1979 Bill, despite its shortcomings, would have taken the first bold step towards freeing the media from Government control. It was doomed when self-seekers pulled down that Government. Now, although the National Front Government had seen through the legislation in its brief span, the result is not too edifying. Public opinion should assert itself to have the law amended at least to drop the provision (Clause 13 - 1 and 2) for a parliamentary committee to breathe down the neck of the proposed Prasar Bharati. Similarly, the ambiguity in the Clause (23-1) providing for issuance of Government directions to the corporation should be removed. Otherwise, the board of directors of the proposed Prasar Bharati will be an exalted Coffee or Tea Board.

The papers included in this volume speak for themselves. Apart from Dr. Ramaswamy R. Iyer who turned the spotlight on the substance of autonomy, Mr O.P. Khushu and Professor. B. N. Koul have dealt with the technical and educational dimensions of electronic media. Mr Khushu, who was then Engineer-in-Chief of All India Radio (now Director, Technical Centre of Asia-Pacific Broadcasting Union) has provided in his paper a rewarding insight into the technical feasibility and cost of decentralised electronic media. Professor Koul who heads the Department of Distance Education at the National Open University has shed light on the potential of the media in promoting non-formal education, a subject completely ignored in the discussion on the Prasar Bharati Bill.

Another professor, Hari Krishna Paranjape, discussed in depth the financial and administrative aspects of autonomy with his characteristic thoroughness. Dr Harish Khanna has brought to bear his vast experience as a civil servant and media professional to highlight the current affairs programmes of the media in the light of the proposals for autonomy. Mr P C Chatterjee who was Director-General of All India Radio and is the author of an authoritative book on broadcasting delineated the organisational structure for autonomous media. Pursuing the topic further, Harsaran Pandey, with her rich experience as a TV producer, examined the practical aspects of autonomy in a down-to-earth manner, with Mr. K.K. Sud, who had risen from the ranks to be the Chief of the News Services Division of All India Radio, highlighting the practical aspects of reporting for the media. Last but not least is the vivid account of media autonomy movements in different countries by Dr. B.S.S. Rao of the National Institute of Rural Development. He has made out an eloquent case for what he called equal opportunity broadcasting.

It is my pleasant duty here to thank all these and other participants in the seminar as well as the Institute of Social Sciences and its affable director, Dr. George Mathew, for giving us an opportunity to discuss the subject in depth.

New Delhi
December 25, 1990.

G S Bhargava

2

Equal Opportunity Broadcasting

B S S Rao

THE theme of equal opportunity broadcasting is developed from two perspectives: (1) accessibility and (2) accountability. Accessibility of the instruments of broadcasting is visualised not only in terms of the reach of airwaves, but also in terms of wider and just participation of the people in the programme output. The accountability of the broadcasters is similarly visualised as responsiveness and answerability in terms of purpose and utility of the programme fare to the audience at large; not restricted to the narrow world of people who constitute the government.

In building this theme, a basic distinction is also envisaged between "Government Service Broadcasting" and "Public Service Broadcasting", based upon our own experiences of the performance of the government media. All government service broadcasting does not become public service broadcasting, and all public service broadcasting need not be supported by, and in support of the government.

The broad political acceptance of the definition of autonomy as partial self-governance and independence as full self-governance is, perhaps, widely understood. But, in the field of broadcasting, the concept of autonomy is largely interpreted to mean unbridled functioning of the electronic media systems, free from government shackles, but within the aegis of the government. Independent broadcasting is associated with private ownership and operation outside the sphere of government. While autonomous broadcasting system is perceived as synonymous with public service broadcasting, independent broadcasting is connected with the commercial system under private enterprise. However, communicationists always believe that the meanings are with the recipients. Based upon these meanings and perceptions, the images are built. Expectations grow out of these images. Therefore, how the meanings are shared in respect of "autonomy", "public service", "independence", "controls" and a host of such usages, becomes critical to the understanding of what is central to the theme of this paper.

Between 1974 and 1987, there have been many Commissions of Inquiry on various issues relating to the management of broadcasting in the Commonwealth countries. Rich material is available in these study reports concerning the broadcasting systems in Britain, Canada, Australia and New Zealand which are considered to be ideal public service broadcasting systems among the democratic countries, favourably matching with our own needs and aspirations. Two other immensely valuable documents of the same period, are the Report of the UNESCO-sponsored International Commission on Communication Problems under the Chairmanship of Sean MacBride and the widely acclaimed Report of the Verghese Panel at home, on Autonomy for Akashvani and Doordarshan.

An endeavour is made to assimilate the thoughts and important recommendations of these national and international committee reports and present their ideas for sharpening my own focus of the theme of Equal Opportunity Broadcasting.

The paper is presented in two parts: Part I reviews the salient recommendations of the following eight documents:

1. Annan Committee Report on Future of Broadcasting in UK (1977);
2. Boyle Committee Report on Canadian Broadcasting Corporation (1977);
3. Verghese Committee Report in India (1978);
4. MacBride Commission (sponsored by UNESCO) on Communication Problems (1980);
5. Dix Committee Report on Australian Broadcasting Commission (1981);
6. Peacock Committee on Funding of Broadcasting in UK (1986);
7. Chapman Commission Report on Broadcasting and Related Telecommunications in New Zealand (1986); and
8. Green Paper on Radio in UK (1987).

Part II of the paper is devoted to build a case for the reconstruction of broadcast media in our country to make them a part of Indian life for the enrichment of the people in cities, towns, villages and forests, providing them equal and just opportunities and wide choices.

1. Annan Committee in UK

A 16-member Committee under the Chairmanship of Lord Annan was appointed by the British Government in April, 1974, to consider the future of broadcasting in UK. The report of the committee was submitted in March, 1977 and its main recommendations on various aspects of broadcasting are reviewed below:[1]

* Traditionally, the State has set for the broadcasters three objectives: entertainment; information and education for large audiences. The Committee added yet another important objective—enrichment—to enlarge people's interests, to carry to them new choices and possibilities in life. The recommendation was that the programmes should create "delight and insight".
* The Committee recommended the setting up of a Local Broadcasting Authority (LBA) to takeover all local Radio stations (after 1979) from BBC and the Independent Broadcasting Authority (IBA). The Local Broadcasting Authority was advised to shoulder responsibility for all local broadcasting services, including cable television. Cable television was envisaged essentially as a local community service and it was recommended that local radio should have mixed sources of finance including advertising.
* The overall suggestion was that Britain should have a three-tier system of broadcasting: the BBC providing national service, the IBA providing regional service and the LBA becoming responsible for local radio.
* The Report recommended no other structural changes in BBC or IBA, or any changes in the manner in which the BBC is financed by the License Fee system.
* The Committee visualised that there would be predominantly more older people and fewer children in Britain by 1990s. More people would be better educated and their demands on broadcasting services would be

different. Hence, it was suggested that broadcasting should be organised as flexibly as possible to adapt to social and technical changes.

* Other important recommendations of the Committee relate to the constitution of a Public Inquiry Board, (at least once in seven years) independent of both Government and the Broadcasting Authorities. The Public Inquiry Board was suggested to hold public hearings and taking a general view of the broadcasting services in the public interest.

Response to the Annan Committee Report

In response to the Report of the Annan Committee, the British Government published a White Paper in July, 1978. The following are some of the main proposals for changes in the constitution, structure and organisation of broadcasting services in UK:

* The Government's principal conclusion was that broadcasting services in UK should continue to be provided as public service and should continue to be the responsibility of public authorities. The concepts of broadcasting Authority and of Public Service Broadcasting have stood the test of time. They should form the foundation for the future.
* The Government also accepted the four requisites for good-broadcasting identified by the Committee—flexibility, diversity, editorial independence and public accountability. However, it observed that editorial freedom carries with it certain obligations which should be exercised responsibly. It is integral to the role of broadcasting authorities that they should be publicly accountable for their trusteeship of the public interest.
* Accepting the Annan Committee recommendation for the setting up of an Open Broadcasting Authority (OBA) to supervise a new service (on the fourth television channel) the Government pointed out that this unique opportunity will be missed if the additional channel is not used to explore the possibilities of programmes which "say something new in new ways". The new channel should provide a significant outlet for programmes which reflect the diversity of cultures including the cultures of the ethnic

minorities and of newcomers to this country.

* The proposal of the Annan Committee to create a new Authority to supervise Local Broadcasting was rejected, and instead the Government permitted both BBC and IBA to expand their local radio services. As a basis for expansion of local radio certain critical criteria were laid down. In this context, it was emphasised that high priority should be given to areas which are relatively deprived in terms of social amenities.

2. Boyle Committee in Canada

The inquiry was undertaken by a Committee of the Canadian Radio-Television and Telecommunications Commission (CRTC) under the Chairman of the Commission—Harry Boyle—at the instance of the Canadian Prime Minister. The Committee appointed in March 1977 against the background of accusations and allegations that CBC programming, especially its French network had a separatist bias, submitted its report in July 1977.[2]

* The Report came out strongly in favour of CBC as the national public service broadcasting organisation in Canada and it felt that it would not be realistic to leave broadcasting to wholly private enterprise. However, the Committee observed that the CBC had failed to facilitate true communication and interaction between English and French-speaking Canadians.
* Pointing out certain deficiencies in the fulfilment of CBC's statutory mandate, the Committee observed: "by over centralising production and programming in Toronto and Montreal and by the orientation of the CBC has failed to serve the special needs of geographic regions".
* By separating the French and English networks into two distinct and isolated services both conceptually and physically, the CBC had failed in its responsibility for actively contributing to the flow and exchange of cultural and regional information and entertainment. And by its heavy dependence on American television programming and excessive reliance on its own internal resources, the CBC had failed to provide for a continuing expression of Canadian identity.

* While agreeing that CBC continues to be the dominant source of television and radio programming in remote and outlying areas of the country, it was emphasised that CBC must provide a alternate and quality programmes in the areas receiving full range of commercial programming. The Committee observed: "it is not the number of people watching such programming but the significance of the programmes to those watching that matters".
* According to the Committee the failure of the CBC to provide adequate communication among the various groups and regions within Canada constituted bias. It pointed out: "Bias is manifested not only when information is distorted but also when essential information is omitted entirely or in part. Bias in this sense which runs counter to the principles of democratic debate, is a form of journalistic malpractice and that must be corrected by CBC if it is to enjoy the confidence of the public and parliament".

Response from the BBC

The President of the CBC reacted sharply to the Report of the Boyle Commission, particularly in respect of the accusation of bias. "To accuse journalists who are making honest editorial judgements of subversiveness because their judgements disagree with some unknown norm is gratuitous and insulting". But, he admitted that CBC was quite aware of its shortcomings and assured that a specific action-plan was prepared to overcome the deficiencies.

Verghese Panel Report

The Working-Group was appointed in August 1977 to look into all aspects of granting autonomy to Akashvani and Doordarshan. It submitted its report in February, 1978 and its illuminating ideas were received with great appreciation in the country. Taking into consideration the tremendous heterogeneity as the most outstanding characteristic of the Indian audience, the Working-Group favoured the creation of a unique statutory body—the National Broadcast Trust (NBT).[3] It was recommended that all the national broadcasting services should be vested exclusively in an independent, impartial and autonomous organisation established by law by parliament to act as a trustee for the national interest.

The restructuring of the electronic media under the Prasar

Bharati Bill as envisaged by the present National Front government is not wholly within the conceptual framework of NBT. It is not proposed here to review in detail the various recommendations of the Verghese Committee even though their relevance is not lost. Some of the most relevant observations of the Committee are cited below:

* Akashvani and Doordarshan combine in themselves the characteristics of marketplace, newspaper, university, national extension agency and cultural academy. As such, a unique institution must enjoy a unique autonomy ... Broadcasting entails no manufacturing or trading functions. Every actual and potential listener or viewer is a consumer and every citizen a share holder. There is no product that can be priced in the market; not any raw materials other than ideas and creative talents. The services rendered or again difficult to quantify: awareness, knowledge, information, pleasure.
* Visualising the future needs, the Committee observed: "While we acknowledge that television is a powerful and effective medium, India should give first priority to the development and densification of radio for at least the next 10-15 years. ... We strongly recommend that Akashvani must develop a determined rural extension thrust which is best done through rapid development of low power local stations".
* Decentralised and participative development from below suggests the need for decentralised messages through local radio and television. The very size and diversity of the country compels movement in this direction.
* In the context of democratising communications the Committee observed: "broadcasting has an equally vital role in making available the information and varied analysis that is the foundation of public opinion which is translated into the sovereign will of the people through democratic debate and elections. The impartiality, accuracy and proficiency of radio and television in catering to the citizens "Right to Know" are therefore, of paramount importance."
* "The tragedy is that Akashvani and Doordarshan have, with rare exception, tended to avoid programmes that specifically

focus on poverty, exploitation, and social justice even if these are linked to educating the illiterate and oppressed about their legal and social rights. The broadcast media have by and large shied from controversy.

4. MacBride Commission

The UNESCO-sponsored International Commission on Communication Problems under the Chairmanship of Sean MacBride was appointed in December 1977 to examine among others the totality of communication problems in the modern society. The final report of the Commission published in June 1980 covers the entire gamut of communication policies and operational systems; and not restricted to broadcasting[4]. Some of the main points of the Report are excerpted below: It is interesting to note that the ideas of the Verghese panel get amply reflected in the recommendations of the Commission.

* Communication is a basic individual right, as well as a collective one required by all communities. Freedom of information—and more specifically the right to seek, impart and receive information—is a fundamental human right.
* Communication is not only a system of information, but also an integral part of development.
* Defence of all human rights is one of the most vital tasks of communication.
* Diversity and choice in the content of communication are a precondition of democratic participation. The development of decentralised and diversified media should provide larger opportunities for a real direct involvement of the people in communication processes.
* The exclusion of disadvantaged groups from normal communication channels is a major issue. Some of these groups in some places are denied such elementary rights to communicate as that of assembly or expression of opinion. Others, more numerous are disfavoured by tradition or dominant social attitudes; this is particularly true of women.
* Development must arise from human growth, the people's confidence in its own strength and social justice. This requires the involvement of the ordinary citizens in decision making as much as possible. Communication should enlarge

the capacity of men and women to take charge of their own development.

* With regard to strengthening of communication capacities, the Commission recommended that a basic radio network should take priority over the development of television, to reach out to illiterate and remote areas. It was the considered opinion of the Commission that utilisation of local radio, low-cost small format television and video system and other appropriate technologies would facilitate production of programmes relevant to community development efforts, stimulate participation and provide opportunity for diversified cultural expression.

5. Dix Committee in Australia

The 4-member Committee appointed by the Australian Government in May, 1979 under the Chairmanship of Alex Dix submitted its Report in June, 1981. This was the first major inquiry into the ABC since it was established as the national public service broadcasting organisation of Australia in 1932[5].

* The Committee recommended reconstruction of ABC into a National Broadcasting Organisation (NBO), which would be responsible for all policy directions. It recommended that greater part of NBO's budget should continue to be funded through parliamentary appropriation. It did not favour the broadcast license fee system. An amendment to the Broadcasting and Television Act was suggested to transfer the power of ownership of all transmitters and associated facilities to the ABC from the Postal system.
* The Committee recommended that the NBO should not be empowered to carry paid commercial advertising. It, however, recommended acceptance of corporate underwriting of its programmes.
* The Committee was highly critical of the ABC for its neglect of the services for Australia's ethnic minorities and aboriginal people.
* The Committee was also very critical of the ABC's failure to reflect the realities of Australian society and its over emphasis on some overseas, particularly British programmes on television at the expense of locally

produced programmes, thus reflecting cultural bias in content.

* The Committee strongly felt that the states and regions should have firmer place in ABC organisation and in the broadcast output. Systems employed for financial devolution and editorial control must reflect the discrete requirements of states and regions. Attention to state and regional variations in the programmes of ABC must be a high priority in the next few years.
* The Committee recommended that the ABC's new charter should express four main objectives for its programmes that they be informative, entertaining, innovative, and directed towards Australian society as a whole and its constituent community groups.
* The Committee proposed that the ABC in cooperation with the commercial stations and Special Broadcast Service should attempt to ameliorate the deprivation in media choice experienced by the Australian rural communities. In this context the reorganisation of the ABC's Radio network with a regional network was recommended to provide country listeners with a range of services equivalent to those in cities.
* The Committee was categorical in its observation that if it is to enjoy new freedoms, the ABC must become more publicly accountable than it had been in the past of many of its activities. It stated: "the issue of accountability and independence are interlocking. If the ABC wishes to spend money provided by the tax payer with minimum restriction in the ways it does so, it must do more than just put excellent programmes on the air".
* The Committee simultaneously favoured more effective exploitation of the avenue earning through imaginative activities such as: marketing of educational/instructional material; patenting of technological development; offering of training programmes; and marketing of film and video cassettes.

Government's Proposals on Reorganisation of ABC

In pursiance of the Dix Committee Report, the Government of Australia issued a clear policy statement on the future development and reorganisation of ABC, in July 1982.

The Government accepted a major portion of the recommendations of the Dix Committee and agreed to rename the Commission as Australian Broadcasting Corporation and provide a statutory charter for ABC. It, however, did not favour the idea of having a National Broadcasting Organisation (NBO) retaining the acronym of ABC. It also rejected the recommendation with regard to corporate under writing of the ABC programmes. The Government reaffirmed the Dix Committee's primary observation that ABC as a publicly funded national organisation must have as its principal responsibility provision of quality service to the community as a whole, and to the parts which make up that whole.

In terms of programme priorities, the Government reiterated the Dix Committee's recommendation that ABC should develop a concern for services in non-metropolitan and isolated areas, and that it should be sensitive to the need for innovation and the enrichment of Australian life, through reflection of minority cultural interests as well as general artistic achievements. "The Government as well as the Australian community want a vigorous, outward looking, confident national broadcaster. The ABC should, therefore, have to more swiftly and surely with the times and not be shackled by convention or traditions which have been overtaken by fast moving developments".

6. Peacock Committee on Financing of BBC

The Report of the 7-member committee under the Chairmanship of Prof. Allan Peacock appointed by the British Government in March 1985 to look into all aspects relating to the Financing of the BBC, was published in July, 1986[6].

* Basing on its inquiry and studies, the Committee concluded that the BBC should continue to be funded by the License Fee System and that it should not accept paid advertisements. It, however, recommended that the License Fee should be indexed on an annual basis to the general rate of inflation. The Committee rejected the idea of advertisements with the critical observation that the main defect of a system based on advertising finance is that the channel owners do not sell programmes to the audience, but audiences to the advertisers. It made the recommendation

that the BBC should take over from the Postal authority the responsibility of collecting and enforcing the payment of broadcast receiver License Fee.

* Two key provisions of the Peacock Committee recommendations are: (a) free market should be supplemented by a subsidised public network administered by a new broadcasting council, to provide programmes of minority or special interests with accent on "knowledge, culture, criticism and experiment". (b) all censorship and wetting should be eliminated because "pre-publication censorship has no place in the free society".
* The Committee visualised a three-stage growth: the first step on the road to a free market system will be to adapt television sets for direct subscription which would replace the License Fee during stage II in the late 1990s, an era of "electronic publishing" in which consumers buy packages of programmes in much the way they buy newspapers.
* To facilitate further deregulation, the Committee favoured abolition of all restrictions on both pay TV systems. It recommended that the British Telecom should be allowed to set up a national cable network, with the national telecommunications systems acting as common carriers for a full range of services, including TV programmes.
* Another important recommendation of the Committee was in relation to the extension of the statutory legislation on obscenity, defamation, blasphemy, sedition and similar matters to cover broadcasting.

Response from BBC

The Chairman of the BBC welcomed the recommendations of the Peacock Committee, particularly the one relating to the indexing of License Fee to the general rate of inflation. The BBC also welcomed the recommendation that it should not be obliged to take advertisements and enter the rating war for additional fun funds.

7. Chapman Committee in New Zealand

The Government of New Zealand appointed a 4-member Royal Commission headed by Prof Robert Chapman in February, 1985 to inquire into Broadcasting and Related Telecommunications in the country. The terms of reference of the Commission included two aspects: (a) suggestion of changes necessary to widen choices and improve the quality of programmes; and (b) how best it can reflect the country's culture and social variety and provide service to all New Zealanders. The Committee submitted its report in September, 1986 and some of the important recommendations are briefly reviewed here.[7]

* The Committee supported the system of public service corporation and recommended that a Broadcasting Corporation (BCNZ) be constituted as a statutory body.
* The Committee preferred the creation of a single body to take care of all broadcasting facilities including cable broadcasting as and when taken up, Telecommunications and auxiliary facilities.
* The Committee laid emphasis on the need for adequate funding of public service broadcasting and recommended increase in the broadcast license fee to a level not less than the annual average subscription to a national newspaper. It was also suggested that this fee should be annually adjusted taking into consideration the rate of inflation.
* The Committee recommended that steps should be taken to provide greater encouragement to local productions for both radio and television, by adopting quota system.
* The Committee examined the aspects relating to the coverage of the aboriginal Maori language and culture and recommended fixing of minimum quotas, if necessary, for increasing the proportion of programming for the Maori-speaking audiences. Similar recommendation was also made to meet the informational needs of the Pacific Island's people.

Even though the Chapman Committee covered a lot of ground and came up with many recommendations, critics were very apprehensive of the results. Doubts were expressed if the Corporation would really make New Zealand a 'democracy of informed citizens' as envisaged by the public service broadcasting. The main criticism was that most of the recommendations were only the nature of cosmetic changes rather than suggesting any structural changes in the system of broadcasting in New Zealand.[8]

8. Green Paper on Radio in Britain

While responding to the recommendations of the Peacock Committee on Financing of BBC, the British Government made a commitment to come up with a separate Green Paper on Radio.[9] This policy document was published in February, 1987.

* The paper made it very clear that the British Government has an open mind and will not hesitate to have structural changes, if necessary, to provide opportunities for more varied radio services and choices to the listeners.
* The Government visualised a scenario permitting operation of three national commercial radio networks and hundreds of local and community radio stations. The BBC is given the green signal and allowed to decide on its own, if it wanted to have its own Local Radio Plans simultaneously with the existing radio networks under its operation.
* The Green Paper was an initiative to open up radio to market forces and back the concept of a strong and varied public service system in UK. The three additional national commercial networks were envisaged by redistribution of available frequencies and transferring a few from BBC without hampering in any way BBC's commitments and obligations.
* The local commercial radio stations were allowed to operate under a "lighter rein" of regulations with regard to both technical standards as well as public service programming. The Government's policy statement envisaging operation of more commercial radio networks was widely welcomed within the BBC and the community of local radio operators.

It is not an easy task to synthesise the valuable ideas of the many scholars who contributed to the wisdom of the commissions of inquiry reviewed earlier, and present anything new and fascinating, conceptually or otherwise. Hence, borrowing the same ideas, an endeavour is made to build a case for a constructed public service broadcasting system in our country. The very approach of reconstruction warrants acceptance of two basic prerequisites: a) openness on the part of the Government as well as people within the establishments of Akashvani and Doordarshan to work for the service of the people—not for their own benefits; and b) a comprehensive pre-understanding of the immediate and long run implications of the changes that are being contemplated. What is required is the commitment to democratise institutions and sustain democracy upholding the high ideals of public service broadcasting.

The plea for reconstruction also assumes a deeper and more emphatic appreciation of the 'why part' of the initiative for multi-dimensional changes in the broadcasting system. I am not going into details of these aspects.

The essential characteristics of Equal Opportunity Broadcasting are visualised as:

1. Widest accessibility of the instruments of broadcasting not in terms of mere availability of signals in the air, but in terms of actual utilisation of the output of the broadcasting centres. This means serving the local people in local language.
2. Making the right to information work, by giving voice to the people to question the broadcasters. The Government servant's approach of the broadcaster that 'I care a damn of what you think of me' should get replaced with 'service to the people' approach.
3. The nation's interests and the interests of the vulnerable sections of society are protected without being traded for commercial earnings to achieve financial viability.
4. Consumer culture and equal opportunity broadcasting do not go together. The electronic media should not contribute to sell me myth that advertising is cost free to the consumers. This is necessary because many of the audiences do not have the perspective to understand how much they contribute to the cost of advertising.
5. Broadcasting organisations should stand out as equal opportunity employers and refuse to give place to unworthy talents. At the same time, the doors of broadcasting should be open to facilitate blossoming of all broadcast talents without bias and favour.

We are accepting the premises that the existing system of broadcasting has not been able to connect itself in any meaningful way with the life of a large proportion of the people in our country.

By virtue of their isolation, social, economic and cultural deprivation the people who share the culture of poverty remained so long willy-nilly outside the frame of reference of the people who managed the affairs of broadcasting. The bias in broadcasting approaches is conspicuous on many accounts. The intent of this paper is to draw attention to the immediate need to end discriminatory approaches and practices in broadcasting and plead for broadcast planning and management based on the needs of democracy. This assumes greater importance when the provision of broadcast services is envisaged as the exclusive responsibility of the public authorities as the custodians of democracy and people's rights. Equal Opportunity Broadcasting (EOB) is suggested as a possible conceptual framework for correcting media inequalities and imbalances bringing the "unheard" and "silent" voices within the fold of broadcasting. This requires basic changes in the perception of programme priorities and a wider perspective of the informational and communication needs of the actual and potential audiences.

As Mark Fowler, past Chairman of the Federal Communications Commission of USA has rightly remarked: "the magic and miracle are not cabined in a box of wires and transistors. The magic and the miracle are to be found in the minds of men and women of free people."[10]

The concept of EOB is developed taking a cue from what Dean Alger calls the need for "the dialogue of democracy". In his well-documented work 'Media and Politics', he warned: If the few who are directly involved in governing primarily talk to the many, rather than maintaining a dialogue with them, after a while there will be alienation and distrust and sooner or later there will be an arrogance of power and then misuse of power by the governing few.[11] Our experiences during the period of Emergency and after need no further elaboration.

Democracy, information spread, choice of options of information gathering and public participation are closely interrelated. In his widely quoted work, *Theory of Democracy Revisited*, Political Scientist and thinker Sartori Giovanni states: "Electoral power *per se* is the mechanical guarantee of democracy, but the substantive guarantee is given by the conditions under which the citizens get the information and exposed to the pressure of opinion makers.[12]

The failure of the broadcast media to forge an effective dialogue in the problems that we are facing today in Kashmir valley, Punjab,

North-East and parts of Assam. The alienation of the dissatisfied groups from the main stream of the Indian society is due the failure of rapport between people and the government and the broadcasting system should particularly feel guilty for having failed to maintain the dialogue of democracy. The distancing of the people and the lack of trust in the instruments is evidently a sign of ill-health of our democracy, not at the people's level but at the level of the state organs.

The reach of the media to all sections of the people dispersed in all regions of the country and the investments on the maintenance of their credibility is always regarded as public investments on democracy. Dick Francis of the BBC Radio once remarked: "the wheels of democracy can quickly grind to a halt without lubrication of knowledge through broadcasting".[13]

The real nature of public service broadcasting and its vitality depend on offering widest choices and in its addressing to the whole community, not parts singled out by education, class or region. The MacBride Report sounded a caution to all nations that communication should no longer be regarded as an incidental service and its development left to chance. "Extension of broadcasting facilities call for new attitudes for overcoming stereotyped thinking and to promote more understanding of diversity and plurality with full respect for the dignity and equality of people living in different conditions and acting in different ways".

Let us have a look at the hard realities. Sometime ago, I attempted an analysis of percentage distribution of air time utilisation on AIR, during 1954-1982 at different time periods and correlate this with our planning priorities. To my surprise, I found that there has been gradual decline in the proportion of time allocated for Special Audience Programmes like rural, tribal, women and children over the years.

The expansion of the AIR network in terms of additions to stations was slow, but significant. The increase in the gross transmission time was also impressive. In terms of average broadcast time per day per station, it increased from hardly 9 hours in 1954 to nearly 13 hours in 1982. With more and more stations coming up, and with an increase in the overall programme output, wider support to development-oriented programmes from AIR was expected. But, my data did not reflect such an assuring trend. In real terms, the broadcast time exclusively designed for rural listeners decreased significantly after mid-seventies, despite the increased stress on agricultural extension and farm production. The rural broadcasts received proportionately more time during the first decade of planning than during later years.[14]

My own studies on television fare in Andhra Pradesh and Pune region of Maharashtra revealed meagre utilisation of television output. A large percentage of the people in interior villages and tribal tracts have no access to television at all. Doordarshan misquotes the reach of TV signals as the reach of the medium. One can see this only as self-deception. The 70 per cent population coverage is a myth.

Doordarshan admits that the programme output on the national network is made available 47 per cent in Hindi, 45 per cent in English and 3 per cent in other Indian languages. That means, people who have no knowledge of Hindi and English languages (who may number about half the population) have no access to the national programmes. A lot of television output is tolerated as unavoidable hammering. If we consider the wastage in the local-oriented, regional service due to lack of connecting cords between needs of life and the message, the wastage is alarming. Nearly one-third of the rural and tribal people in Maharashtra region were found to be non-watchers of television, even though facilities for TV viewing were available. The reason was that the programmes were no meaningfully connected to the people's occupation—their way of life.[15]

Public accountability gets best reflected in the rapport that the broadcast media maintains with the public. If the public are indifferent to the affairs of the media, it is a sad reflection that the media are unconcerned with the public. If the broadcast systems hold the public in high esteem and make a best effort to provide them services with equal concern and respect to all sections of the audience, irrespective of their power to mobilise vocal support, then automatically, the broadcasting organisations gain public confidence and respect.

Public accountability can be ensured by involving public in programme planning as well as scrutiny through effective monitoring and evaluation of the programmes by non-governmental and credible public institutions. All reports generated within the organisations of radio and television (by the Audience Research Units) and external bodies should be free from the seal of confidentiality. They should be public documents, open to public reading and response. The annual reports of the broadcasting organisations should invariably carry a detailed account of complaints received on policy issues and denial of information rights.

Direction-based programming and ritual-based programming should get replaced with need-based programming determined on the basis of studies and public inquiries. However, audience needs may not always match with state requirements. In this context, the programming needs, have to be based on the principle of "common good".

The selling of audiences to the advertisers and the sponsors, whether by autonomous organisations or by private broadcasters, leads to the same results. Social scientists strongly believe that commercial broadcasting specifically under conditions of non-availability of wider choices, has disastrous consequences leading to crippling of the mind and loss of power to think and act. The economic consequence is concentration of market power ultimately leading to oligopoly/monopoly. As an industrial nation we are in the take off stage, with problems of adjustment to the unchecked flow of product selling and brain washing messages. The rural community which had the advantage of geographical isolation was enjoying a natural insulation against commercialism. With commercialisation of radio and television, this protective ring is getting fast broken up. The commercial interests are penetrating the rural homes with propaganda techniques to take best advantage in terms of boosting up of their corporate earnings. The public service broadcasting organisations should resist getting sold off to commercial interests as it is detrimental to the interests of innocent and captive audiences.

Another aspect of commercialisation of programme output is much more serious. Majority of the programme personnel develop a vested interest and start looking for earning something extra through manipulation of air-time for commercial broadcasting. A trading approach gets developed in all aspects of programming, leading to submerging of audience interests to commercial interests and personal interests.

A careful reconsideration of the commercialisation aspect is, therefore, suggested as it negates the concept of equal opportunity broadcasting.

One more dimension of Equal Opportunity Broadcasting, is the need for better opportunities of employment within the broadcasting system based upon the principles of professional equality and justice. The ad-hocism in the utilisation of talents and unplanned growth unrelated to requirements of staff and their training, have brought into sharp focus the allegations of induction of unworthy elements through backdoors. Equal Opportunity-based entry system and growth linked to demonstrated abilities should receive immediate attention.

The allegations of favouritism and corruption in talent hunting and utilisation for programme generation need to be looked into on priority basis to boost up the morale of the staff. Fair and sound screening systems and methods of evaluation need to be evolved to give a stature to the establishment as Equal Opportunity Employers. Simultaneously, evolution of sound manpower recruitment systems and growth-oriented Human Resource Development practices matching to the requirements of creative and professional organisations, not rigidly tied to hierarchy-oriented bureaucratic establishments should receive serious attention.

Action-Points

Towards operationalisation of the concept of Equal Opportunity Broadcasting, the following action-points are suggested:

1. Top priority needs to be given for the spread of radio, specifically the local radio stations to facilitate easy access and wider participation of the community. This would help establish identity and promote integration.
2. More air-time for specific audiences like rural/tribal, women and such other information-deprived categories to provide them "delight and insight".
3. Linking of all low-power TV relay kendras with the nearest regional centre and closing down of relay centres fed exclusively from New Delhi to stop "master-servant" linkages.
4. Lighter reins of control on local and regional programming: This requires democratisation of the media operations by loosening controls from headquarters in auditions, talent utilisation, etc. Except where major policy issues are involved, the Regional Centres, serving specific sub-cultures, should be free to chalk out their own

programming pattern.

5. Encouragement of independent and objective studies on broadcasting by external organisations and publication of all reports of broadcasting generated within, by the Audience Research wings, as well as external organisations without any seal of confidentially.
6. Persuasive orientation training to enlarge the vision of broadcasting personnel. Both learning and unlearning are needed to grasp the various dimensions of broadcast needs, ways and means to cultivate responsiveness to the audience, and gaining trust and patronage from various sections.
7. Commercialisation should be subject to tighter scrutiny and control, to check the spread of consumerism. At the same time, more social selling through innovative programming to give wider support to rural-oriented arts, skills providing sustenance, and reflecting the creativity of the people is needed. The spirit behind broadcasting should be to promote faithfully the Indianness. It should be a national endeavour to make best use of the broadcasting institutions, without being totally commercial, to project the varied dimensions of India as a great country of many people.

REFERENCES

1. Future of Broadcasting in UK, Annan Committee Report, *Combroad* (quarterly Journal o: the Commonwealth Broadcasting Association), London, Issue No. 35, April, 19 '7.
2. Report f Inquiry into the Canadian Broadcasting Corporation, *Combroad*, Londoı Issue No. 36, July, 1977.
3. Gov·ınment of India (1978), Akash Bharati (Volume I), Report of the Working Grc up on Autonomy for Akashvani and Doordarshan, New Delhi, Ministry of Information and Broadcasting.
4. UNESCO (1980), Many Voices One World, Report of the International Commission for the Study of Communication Problems, Paris.
5. Report of the Commission of Inquiry into the ABC, *Combroad*, London, Issue No. 52, July, 1981.
6. Report of the Committee on Financing the BBC, *Combroad*, London, Issue No. 72, September, 1986.
7. Report of the Royal Commission of the Inquiry: Broadcasting and Related Communications in New Zealand, *Combroad*, London, Issue No. 74, January, 1987.
8. David Beatson, Commission of Inquiry into Broadcasting in New Zealand, *Combroad*, London, June, 1987.
9. Green Paper on Radio in Britain, *Combroad*, London, Issue No. 75, June, 1987.
10. Fowler's address to the American National Association of Broadcasters, Dallas (1987), Reported in *Combroad*, Issue No. 75, June, 1987.

11. Alger, Dean. E (1989), The Media and Politics, Prentice Hall, New Jersey. Eaglewood Cliffs.
12. Sartori Giovanni (1987), The Theory of Democracy Revised, Volume I, Chattan, Chattan House, NJ.
13. Dick Francie, "Public Service Broadcasting will Survive", *Combroad*, Issue No. 65, December, 1984.
14. Rao, BSS, Development Priorities and Programme Pattern in AIR, *Vidura*, Volume 20(2), August, 1983.
15. —— (1980) Television for Rural Development—A Study in Maharashtra (unpublished Ph.D Thesis) Pune, Pune University.

3

Autonomy: Form and Substance

Ramaswamy R. Iyer

I

IN the context of the discussion about media autonomy, it may be be useful to devote some thought to the nature of autonomy and the difference between form and substance. Autonomous bodies are not new things in this country: we have considerable experience of establishing and operating what are known as 'autonomous institutions'. In the light of that experience we have to consider what autonomy means; what we are trying to achieve and through what means; and what successes or failures we have had. I am not an expert on the media, and shall not be dealing with issues specific to All India Radio or Doordarshan; I shall be mainly concerned with the concept of autonomy and the means of making it effective.

II

Autonomy can mean several things. On some occasions, when we talk about autonomous bodies we mean merely that these are bodies outside the Government with a legal existence of their own. In some other contexts we refer to autonomy in the sense of administrative and financial autonomy, namely the ability of an institution or an organisation to run its own affairs, that is to say, appoint its own personnel, operate its own bank accounts, enter into contracts, make purchases, incur expenditure, and so on. We may also think of autonomy in the sense of professional or functional autonomy, that is to say, independence in the discharge of the entrusted functions. In the use of the word 'autonomy' the different senses are not always kept distinct, but we must remember that they do not always or necessarily go together. Functional autonomy is of course the most important: legal and administrative autonomies are only aids to this. We can have instances of functional autonomy without legal or administrative autonomy and *vice versa*.

We have a wide range of institutions and organisations all of which can be brought under the rubric of 'autonomous institutions': for instance the judiciary; the Comptroller and Auditor General of India; the Union Public Service Commission; the Reserve Bank of India; the nationalised banks and public financial institutions; the Chief Election Commissioner; the Central Vigilance Commissioner; registered societies established by the Government for various purposes such as the Council of Scientific and Industrial Research, the Indian Council of Agricultural Research, the National Institute of Hydrology, the National Water Development Agency, etc.; statutory bodies such as certain Boards; and of course, public enterprises (whether established in the form of corporations by statute or as companies under the Companies Act). Broadly speaking, these can be grouped into two groups, namely, (i) those which are a part of the governmental machinery and function in accordance with governmental rules and procedures, but which are autonomous in the sense of having been made independent in the discharge of their essential professional or other specialised functions; and (ii) those which are legal entities outside the Government having the form of statutory corporations or Boards or Commissions or Government Companies or registered societies. (Incidentally, we cannot always guess the legal status of an institution from its name.) The autonomy of institutions in both the groups mentioned varies considerably in kind and degree; and many of them are subject to different degrees of governmental influence and control. The important point is that such differences cannot be directly related to their legal form. Let us go into this in some detail.

III

The judiciary is in a class by itself. It is part of the Government but not a part of the *Executive* Government: it is a distinct and parallel organ of government. It is substantially independent of the Executive wing in administrative and financial matters; but the Finance Ministry does play a role in approving its major capital expenditure schemes, and the integration of its budget into the total Government budget. Its financial powers, therefore, cannot be said to be absolute. In so far as its judicial functions are concerned its decisions and rulings are of course binding on the Executive Government. Nevertheless, in practice there have been instances which seem to suggest that some elements in the judiciary have allowed themselves to be unduly influenced by the Executive Government. The judiciary is supposed to be a bulwark of liberties, but it did not effectively stand up to the Executive when civil liberties and fundamental rights were abridged during the period of the Emergency; there seemed to have been a failure of nerve on the part of the judiciary at that time. Perhaps it was a question of personalities and their amenability to pressure or influence. It must be added that the Executive Government had one effective instrument in its hands, namely, the power to transfer judges to remote places. It will be seen therefore that even the independence of the judiciary, by which we set much store, has in practice been less than absolute. In general, however, it can be (theoretically) said to be the exemplar of autonomy.

IV

The CAG of India, the Union Public Service Commission, and the Chief Election Commissioner fall into one category; they are all constitutional authorities. Their autonomy derives from the fact that they have constitutional responsibilities to discharge. They also share another guarantee of autonomy, namely, a stable tenure of appointment and non-removability except in accordance with an elaborate and difficult procedure. Yet another measure of ensuring independence is to make a functionary ineligible for further appointment under the Government after his term of office, but in this respect the position is not uniform. While the CAG cannot be appointed to any post under the Central or a State Government after his term of office, such a prohibition does not exist in the case of the judiciary or the Chief Election Commissioner. We all know that retired judges are being appointed as chairmen of commissions and committees, and there was also an instance of a retired judge of a High Court being appointed as India's Ambassador to the USA; and a former Chief Election Commissioner was appointed as the Governor of a State. However, we are not concerned with these differences in the present context. The important fact is that all these authorities enjoy full functional autonomy in the sense that they have a constitutional obligation and right to discharge certain functions; the Executive Government cannot prevent them from discharging such functions, nor can it bypass these institutions. The recommendations of the UPSC and the observations of the CAG have to be given due consideration by the Government, and there are procedures for bringing any deviation or non-compliance or non-acceptance to the notice of Parliament. The CAG also enjoys substantial administrative powers. In financial matters the CAG enjoys the same powers as any of the administrative Ministries. This means that in matters going beyond the powers of the administrative Ministries he has to seek the concurrence of the Finance Ministry; similarly, the overall budget proposals of the Audit Department do undergo some scrutiny in the Finance Ministry before incorporation into the Government's budget. To this extent it can be said that the CAG is not totally independent of the Executive Government in regard to administrative and financial matters, but this cannot be regarded as a serious abridgement of his autonomy

The Central Vigilance Commissioner falls into a different category. This is an institution created by a Government resolution and it has no Constitutional or statutory backing. However, the Government have deliberately and voluntarily granted functional autonomy to the CVC by providing a guaranteed tenure to the incumbent, and requiring a report to be made to Parliament regarding cases of non-acceptance of the CVC's recommendations. This is a somewhat fragile autonomy as it can at any time be rescinded or modified by a new Government resolution, though this would undoubtedly attract a great deal of adverse attention. There are provisions in the Government resolution relating to the Central Vigilance Commission under which the Central Government can in the public interest extend the initial three-year term of the CVC for a further period of up to two years, and may in exceptional circumstances allow the CVC to accept further employment under the Union or a State Government or any political public office. These provisions perhaps dilute the autonomy of the CVC to some extent.

The Atomic Energy Commission is merely a body established by a Government resolution and is very much a part of the Government and not a separate legal entity. However, through special arrangements this organisation enjoys substantially higher administrative and financial powers than other Ministries of the Government, and has also been exempted from some of the procedural requirements to which Government offices in general are subject. However, this is a special case.

The Board of Industrial and Financial Reconstruction (BIFR) is a body set up by a statute, which exercises quasi-judicial powers, and has a large measure of administrative and financial autonomy. Its Chairman and Members have also been given guaranteed tenures. However, it has not been made a body corporate and is not a legal entity outside the Government. The salaries and allowances of the Chairman and Members are defrayed out of the Consolidated Fund of India, and the BIFR functions in accordance with governmental rules and procedures, like any other government office. The Chairman has the powers of a Ministry and the Secretary those of the Head of a Department. The BIFR is thus administratively and financially a part of the Government but is functionally independent.

V

What we have been considering so far is a group of institutions within the governmental structure, with varying degrees of administrative and financial autonomy but with substantial functional autonomy; and the functional autonomy in these cases derives not from the establishment of legal entities outside the Government but from specific provisions of the Constitution or the relevant statute or Government resolution. Turning now to bodies with a separate legal existence outside the Government, the CSIR and the ICAR are again special cases. They are both outside the Government and a part of the Government. In so far as they are registered societies with a legal existence of their own, they are outside the Government, and their affairs are managed by their governing bodies. Nominally, there are separate Government Departments corresponding to these organisations, but the Directors-General of the ICAR and CSIR also double as Secretaries to the Government in the Department of Agricultural Research and Education and Scientific and Industrial Research respectively. For all practical purposes, therefore, these bodies are virtually part of the Government and function like Government departments. Some minor advantages arise from their registered-society form, but they are too closely integrated with the Government to be really regarded as autonomous bodies outside the Government. As mentioned earlier, they are special cases and do not really serve as useful models for a consideration of the question of grant of autonomy to an institution.

Apart from the ICAR and the CSIR we have a large number of other registered societies established by the Government, for instance bodies like the National Water Development Agency and the National Institute of Hydrology attached to the Ministry of Water Resources. These are autonomous only in the sense that they are legal entities outside the Government, with governing bodies of their own. In practical terms, however, these organisations hardly enjoy any degree of autonomy, whether functional or administrative or financial. Their governing bodies are heavily dominated by Government officials, and they require governmental approvals, and in particular the Finance Ministry's concurrence, for practically any decision of importance. For all practical purposes, they are subordinate offices of the Ministries to which they are attached. Their autonomy is confined to contingent expenditure, minor purchases, and the appointment of the lower staff.

VI

Finally, we come to public enterprises. A few of them are corporations set up by statutes, but most of them are companies established under the Companies Act. They are very clearly not part of the Government. They have deliberately been distanced from the Government through the grant of corporate form and the establishment of legal entities outside the Government. In theory they are fully autonomous; and yet the most troublesome question in relation to public enterprises is that of autonomy. Almost four decades after we began establishing corporate public enterprises, the major complaint of public enterprise managements continues to be that of excessive bureaucratic and political interference and a lack of adequate autonomy. The question of autonomy is at the heart of the public enterprise debate. We have not so far been able to resolve the conundrum of the combination of managerial autonomy for public enterprises with a proper functional relationship with the Government.

There are numerous complaints from public enterprise managements regarding the difficulties experienced in their relationship with the Government. However, while these are important, what public enterprise managements have in mind when they complain about the relationship with the Government is (a) something intangible, which we may loosely describe as 'the quality of the relationship'; and (b) the tangle of informal relationships, inter-actions and interferences.

What do we mean by 'the quality of the relationship'? The first point to note here is that even though we have got away from the old system of departmental undertakings and have moved over to the establishment of legal entities with corporate form, old ideas and attitudes persist, and the Government tends to continue to regard public enterprises as subordinate offices. Strangely enough, even modern ideas of management like Information Systems have had the effect of aggravating this tendency. The Government tends to establish elaborate information systems calling for all kinds of information which should normally go only to the Boards of Directors. There is also a tendency to multiply reports and returns, call for them at short intervals, hold numerous monitoring and review meetings (as well as other special meetings) and in general function in such a manner that the distinction between monitoring and management is lost sight of. Governmental requirements are so multifarious and the necessity for governmental approval so frequent that many Chief Executives located outside Delhi have to make several trips to Delhi every month for one purpose or another. The fact of the matter is that parliamentary requirements, governmental requirements for planning and policy-formulation and the requirements of monitoring, all tend to reinforce the tendency of any bureaucracy to increase its power, and this creates a relationship of superior and subordinate between the Ministry and public enterprises. Even a junior official in the Ministry, while dealing with public enterprises, feels that he speaks on behalf and with the authority of the Government. Many of the problems which public enterprises complain about—what we may call the grit in the interface—is due to this fact.

Turning to informal relationships and interferences, these are of many kinds, some proper and some improper. For instance, both the Ministers and the higher levels of the bureaucracy (and indeed even the lower levels) tend to make excessive demands on certain facilities which are much more readily available in public enterprises than within the governmental machinery. What is far more irksome, and an impediment to good management, is informal interference and pressures in matters such as appointments, transfers, nominations for training programmes abroad, disciplinary matters, the awards of contracts or agencies or dealerships, and so on. This kind of informal interference, which may take place through telephone calls, casual hints during private meetings or at lunches or dinners or sometimes even through letters, can play havoc with the management. Informal influence or pressure may also be brought to bear on public enterprises in regard to major matters like investment decisions or location decisions, and sometimes even the choice of technology or the selection of consultants or prime contractors. Needless to say, such interferences cause a serious erosion of managerial autonomy and consequently also a serious abridgement of their accountability; they also tend to deprofessionalise the decision-making process in public enterprises.

There have been a number of attempts to bring about the needed changes in the relationship between the Government and public enterprises. In the present context we are not concerned with those reforms. What we have to note is the fact that despite their corporate form and their theoretical possession of ample powers, it has not been possible to ensure the operational autonomy of public enterprises, and that this continues to be the major problem in relation to their performance. (Incidentally, there have been references of late to the need to strengthen the autonomy of the Reserve Bank of India and the public financial institutions. One would have thought that these were already autonomous! This merely goes to show that formal autonomy does not necessarily mean effective practical autonomy.)

VII

From the foregoing survey and analysis, certain conclusions follow. The first is that on the one hand legal autonomy is not a guarantee of functional or operational autonomy; and that on the other, it is possible to evolve conventions of functional autonomy even in the absence of legal autonomy. On the whole, however, legal autonomy is indeed very useful even though it may not be adequate in itself. The provision of a statutory backing to the Broadcasting Corporation of India is therefore to be welcomed, though much more needs to be done.

Secondly, quite apart from institutional arrangements, a great deal depends on the top personnel in charge. The selection of the right Chief Executive and the manning of the top-level management body (i.e., the Prasar Bharati Board) is a matter of the utmost importance. For this purpose, it is not enough merely to transfer the responsibility for selection from the Government to a separate body; such a step merely pushes the question one stage further. Whether the Government does the selection itself or entrusts it to a separate high-level body, what is needed is a fully objective and professional process of formulation of job-specifications, definition of criteria, short-listing and actual selection, with (if necessary) expert professional assistance.

Thirdly, the selected Chief Executive and Board Members have to be given a guaranteed tenure, and should not be easily removable during the period of their tenure. This has been taken care of in the legislation.

Fourthly, we have to avoid the kind of erosion of autonomy which has taken place in public enterprises. The organisation should be left to be managed and operated by its own management, and the kind of day-to-day involvement of and interference by the Government (whether at the political or bureaucratic level) which has become universal in the case of public enterprises, should be strictly avoided. Institutional arrangements alone cannot ensure this; there has to be voluntary self-restraint on the part of the Government at both the political and the bureaucratic levels. This is a matter of establishing healthy conventions and maintaining them scrupulously.

Fifthly, the autonomy of the proposed organisation should not become a mere legal fiction, as has happened in the case of numerous registered societies which virtually function as subordinate offices of the Government. This may appear unlikely in this case in view of the high-level governing body which has been provided for and the provisions relating to their tenure and unremovability. However, there are provisions in the Bill which could eventually lead to excessive bureaucratic control.

For instance, the power of making rules for carrying out the provisions of the Act will vest in the Central Government. This is understandable, but the matters in respect of which the Government will make rules cover all kinds of administrative detail which could well have been left to the Corporation.

The extent to which the Corporation will have financial independence also seems very doubtful. If the funds are going to be provided mainly by the Government, some governmental scrutiny at the budget stage would be unavoidable, but one is not sure whether this will be a broad scrutiny limited to overall magnitudes, or will become a detailed scrutiny of programmes and activities, which will reintroduce control by the Government through the back door: one fears that the latter is likely to happen. If indeed the intention is to make the Corporation a high-level autonomous body, then the

Government should not really proceed beyond the setting of a limit to the funding, and should be willing to leave the programmes and activities to be determined entirely by the Corporation. Further, the legislation does not even leave it to the Corporation to manage its own surplus funds: the investment of these funds has to be 'prescribed' by the Government. While this may be necessary in the case of organisations like the LIC or the UTI, considering the magnitude of their operations and the impact they may have on the capital market and of course the safety of the individual subscribers' funds, it is not clear why such a provision is considered necessary in the case of Prasar Bharati. It would appear that in regard to financial matters Prasar Bharati will be definitely less autonomous than public enterprises which do not have to submit their budgets to the Government (except that their capital outlay programmes come under discussion as part of the national planning process) and which are left to invest their own surplus funds in such securities as they consider appropriate.

There are yet other provisions which limit the autonomy of the Corporation. In the case of public enterprises the Government appoints the Chief Executive and the Board of Directors and all appointments below the Board level are left entirely to the public enterprises themselves, which is as it should be, as personnel planning and management is one of the important aspects of managerial autonomy. The legislation not merely provides for the appointment of the Chairman and the members of the Board but also lays down how the Corporation should appoint its employees: there are provisions which require Recruitment Boards to be set up. The qualifications and conditions of service of the members constituting the Recruitment Board have to be 'prescribed', i.e., laid down by rules to be made by the Government.

These provisions regarding the budget, the investment of funds, Recruitment Boards, etc., have the potential over the years of both severely limiting the autonomy of the Corporation and bureaucratising its functioning.

Lastly, while AIR and Doordarshan should be fair and objective in their presentation of information, and will need functional autonomy for this purpose, we must remember that the Government will also need a vehicle through which it can disseminate its socio-economic policies and programmes, and propagate certain objectives. Clearly, AIR and Doordarshan are now functioning both as information media and as vehicles through which the programmes and policies of the Government are published and propagated. If the Corporation has to play two distinct roles, namely, the media role and the role of a publicity vehicle for the national plan programmes and socio-economic policies and objectives, some degree of informal interaction between the Government and the Corporation will be very necessary. If so, it is a matter of considerable importance to ensure that these informal interactions do not get vitiated either by excessive bureaucratic interference (as in the case of public enterprises) or by an excessive assertion of autonomy by the Corporation. It is difficult to form a clear idea from the provisions of the legislation as to how precisely the relationship between the Government and the Corporation in this regard will evolve.

It will also be necessary to ensure that while seeking autonomy from the Government, AIR and Doordarshan do not come within the undue influence of private organisations which sponsor programmes and are important sources of revenues. However, these are matters which cannot be gone into here; the present paper has been concerned mainly with the idea of autonomy and how to make it a reality.

POSTSCRIPT

The above is a slightly abridged version of a paper presented at the seminar organised by the Institute of Social Sciences on April 28, 1990. Since then, the Prasar Bharati Bill has undergone some changes, and has been passed by Parliament and has become an Act. Unfortunately, the fears expressed earlier about the autonomy of Prasar Bharati being formal rather than real continue to remain valid.

The provisions for governmental approval to the Corporation's budget (Section 20), the manner in which the bureaucracy is actually likely to release the approved funds, the kind of "scrutiny" which is likely to take place in this context, and the Government's right to seek information (Section 24) are together likely to hamstring and bureaucratise the Corporation's functioning and seriously erode its autonomy. The Government's control over the quantum of broadcasting time which can be devoted to advertisements (Section 12(5)) and the quantum of fees and charges which the Corporation can levy (Section 12(7)) means that the Corporation cannot hope to become financially self-reliant but will continue to be dependent heavily on Government funding. On the personnel front, the Corporation's professional and managerial freedom is likely to be seriously constrained by the need to consult a statutory Recruitment Board (Section 10). In respect of both financial and personnel matters it seems clear that Prasar Bharati will be much less autonomous than public enterprises, though even these have been complaining about inadequate autonomy.

In terms of Section 33, regulations in regard to personnel matters framed by the Corporation will be subject to Government approval; and *all* the regulations made by the Corporation, on whatever subject matter and howsoever operational in nature, have to be placed before Parliament and are subject to ratification, modification or annulment by Parliament (Section 34). The theory of 'subordinate legislation' seems to have been carried very far indeed.

One guarantee of autonomy, namely, a stability of tenure for the Chairman and Members of the Board and a difficult procedure for their removal, certainly exists in the Act. However, this is somewhat weakened by the provision for the wholesale supersession of the Board which has been introduced. This requires a reference to Parliament, but this should present no serious difficulty to a Government which has a good majority in Parliament; and this "protection" from arbitrary executive action is achieved only by involving Parliament in executive decision-making, which seems quite inappropriate.

It would appear that neither the Government nor Parliament was willing to repose any confidence or trust in the very high-level body which they were establishing. This is clearly evident from the superimposition on top of Prasar Bharati of two different reviewing bodies, namely, the Broadcasting Council and a Parliamentary Committee. All bodies which are substantially funded by Government are necessarily within the purview of Parliament, particularly when they are also subject to audit by the CAG, and it could have been left to Parliament to establish a Committee to look into Prasar Bharati's functioning if it so desired, in the same way as it has established other Committees such as the Committee on Public Undertakings. The incorporation of a provision for a Parliamentary Committee in the Prasar Bharati Act itself virtually makes that Committee a part of the executive structure of Prasar Bharati; the propriety of this seems very doubtful. The Broadcasting

Council, which will have a full-time President [Section 14 (3)], will not merely receive and deal with complaints but is also empowered to advise the Corporation on the discharge of its functions. Since the Parliamentary Committee can also make recommendations in regard to the discharge of its functions by the Corporation, there is clearly the possibility of a conflict between the advice of the Broadcasting Council and the recommendations of the Parliamentary Committee; and the conflict could be complicated by the fact that the Broadcasting Council will include four Members of Parliament.

Apart from the question of autonomy, what emerges from a perusal of the Act is that the system which is being set up is going to be a cumbersome one to operate. Not only will the Corporation be negotiating throughout the year with the bureaucracy for the release of funds, obtaining the Government's approval and Parliamentary ratification for the regulations that it makes from time to time, dealing with advice from the Broadcasting Council and recommendations from the Parliamentary Committees, and so on; but even the functioning of its own Board may present serious problems. The Prasar Bharati Board will be a large one with a very diverse membership, and the majority principle may not prove easy to operate in practice. The provisions for the representation of employees (divided into two categories, namely, the engineering staff and the others, with no special concern for professionals other than engineers and with common elections in which all employees from the seniormost managers to the unskilled workers will participate) may present difficult operational problems.

After all the seminars, newspaper articles, debates and discussions, what has been created seems a clumsy and unworkable system. It would not be surprising if within a very short period everyone looks back with regret to the period when AIR and DD were departments of Government!

4

Need for Competition

H K Paranjape

THE Prasar Bharati Bill has been presented in fulfilment of the National Front's promise of ensuring genuine autonomy to the electronic media. A question that needs to be initially examined in this context is why there has been so much dissatisfaction with the way the broadcasting media have been working, and what are the changes that many of us want, what are the objectives that we expect to attain, through the media autonomy.

What many of us want to ensure is that the broadcasting media being powerful tools of education and communication, should be so used as to promote to the maximum possible extent the cultural, educational and socio-political needs of our society. In this context it should not be overlooked that we are a very large country with many languages, and with many cultural streams intermingling with each other. We are also a poor country where illiteracy still exists among large sections of the people. The audio and the audio-visual media have therefore even a more critical role to play in our society than in better placed ones. At the same time, it should not be overlooked that, while a local radio set is now within the reach of almost everybody who has some regular income, the normal price of a TV set in the country is over three times our per capita annual income. Therefore, if the TV programmes have to reach a substantial number of people, not only shall we have to wait for quite some time even if maximum attempts are made to produce TV sets on a large scale so as to make them available cheap—for the bulk of our people to possess their own TV sets, but even the provision of a community set to practically all the villages and localities in the country is going to take quite some years and much investment.

That is why the oft-cited BBC is a wrong example to keep in mind when we think of the kind of organisation we need. The UK is a small country, largely homogeneous in character. We should also not forget that the BBC has no longer a monopoly; other agencies have been set up to offer competition. Moreover, not only are the external broadcasts of the BBC very much under the guidance of the Government but the BBC is also known to be part of the British Establishment, and has not much to show by way of programmes unacceptable to the ruling groups. What has however been important for its reputation has been the credibility it has been able to establish for its comparative objectivity, especially where British and other interests clash. It is obvious that those who control the BBC have had an understanding about how to preserve this reputation and its importance unlike those who have controlled the media in India.

In our context, it appears to me that one monolithic corporation would hardly be able to ensure the attainment of the above mentioned objectives. It is not as if we have no experience of 'autonomous' corporations. We have had a plethora of them—the Reserve Bank, the State Bank, other banks, the LIC, Indian Airlines, State Transport, Electricity Boards, and so many Government companies. Can one say that any of these have been able to operate with genuine autonomy, whatever their legal position? Why should we then think that the proposed Prasar Bharati will be different?

The idea that by giving some kind of a non-removable status to those in charge, we shall ensure a full play to all the different streams of culture, information, and ways of thinking is to believe in a mirage. What we need for some genuine free play for different ways of using the media and different schools of thought is competition. True that, with broadcasting being a very capital heavy service, and also with the technical limitations regarding available wave lengths and channels, the number of competing agencies will be small. But expecting full objectivity and a free play for various streams of thinking and information from a single monolithic corporation is to expect a miracle. No one set of persons, however capable and well intentioned they may be, can ensure this.

I would suggest the following kind of set-up to provide a reasonable degree of competition, and also ensure the possibility of the programmes being related to the genuine requirements of the various cultural and regional streams in our country:

a. We should have one *technical corporation*, set up by the Government of India, to provide the hardware for broadcasting throughout the country. This is where the largest part of the investment comes in, and also where the technical as well as personnel economies of scale are likely to be large. The task of this corporation will be to provide the hardware and make broadcasting facilities available *on contract* to the various programme corporations which are set up in the country. The corporation should be under a legal obligation to provide fair opportunities on a cost-plus minimum returns basis to all the programme corporations set up under below. To ensure that this corporation treats all programme corporations fairly, a code governing the relationship should be laid down by law, after consultation with the Inter-State Council, and by a two-thirds majority in the Rajya Sabha.

b. The *programme corporations* should be envisaged at three levels: (i) those set up by the Government of India; (ii) those set up by the State Governments, at least one in each State; and (iii) those which may be set up by the local bodies, universities and other public institutions.

What I envisage is that the Central corporation can provide programmes, as now, for the whole country. Facilities should be available to it to broadcast both nation-wide and regional types of programmes in each region, with at least one wavelength and one channel allotted to it for the purpose. The State corporation(s) would be expected to broadcast within the State; and the local body or the university agencies would be expected to broadcast only in the given locality. This does not preclude one programme agency from deciding by agreement to simultaneously broadcast a programme which is scheduled by another. Alternatively, re-broadcasting of programmes shown elsewhere should also be permitted.

The main purpose of having such independent corporations is to give maximum scope not only to India's diverse traditions in the cultural and linguistic fields but also to ensure that talent from different parts of the country has equal and adequate scope because of the competition among different corporations. Today, especially when it comes to news and discussion features as well as talks, the maximum scope in these is available to those located in Delhi. Almost every event in Delhi gets projected in the national news while similar events in other parts of the country are overlooked; discussions and talks are mainly monopolised by those located in Delhi as if talent for such purposes is rarely available elsewhere in the country. The present system also makes it obligatory for the listeners and viewers compulsorily to attend to programmes in Hindi or English which quite a large number among them cannot follow or appreciate. While this facility should be open to everybody in the country, it is essential for a multilingual country like ours that a listener or a viewer has a choice between a programme in Hindi/English and a programme in his own language.

A question would immediately be put as to whether this is economically feasible. There should be no difficulty at all on the radio side. For television, obviously, additional investment will be necessary. The Planning Commission will have to be asked to look into the matter. If any credence is to be given to their approach of decentralised planning and development, it is quite obvious that the programmes for each region and locality will have to be attempted to be related to the felt needs of that society, region and locality. This will only be possible with the kind of set-up envisaged here. Moreover, for a very large section of our people, the most effective method of providing education and information would obviously be through these media. Adequate investment in these facilities should therefore receive high priority in our plans. If regional and district agencies are to play a genuinely large role in development and administration, decentralised programme-provision has surely to be encouraged.

An important requirement of these corporations to be able to pursue their ideas freely is that they must be financially viable. The sources of revenue would include the following:

a. Licence fee—A very unfortunate decision was thoughtlessly taken some years back to abolish the licence fee. While a fee may be now unenforceable in the case of radios, it would be quite practicable to reimpose the licence fee for TV sets. A person—or an agency—who spends over Rs. 10,000—for buying a set can surely afford to spend a hundred or two hundred rupees as fee per year. Moreover, this way he can be given a choice to show his preference among the different programme agencies; his first choice can receive, say, 45 per cent, the second one 30 per cent, and the third one 25 per cent of what he pays.

b. Advertisement revenue—This is obviously the largest single source of revenue for the broadcasting media. One advantage of having competing programme agencies will be that the advertisers also will have a choice about which programme agencies they will patronise, and how much. True that there can be unhealthy competition among programme corporations to obtain advertisement revenue; but these corporations will be restrained in this matter by the provisions regarding unfair trade practices mentioned below, and broadcasting council which will ensure that their programmes do not transgress a code of conduct which will be laid down.

   A new dimension to advertisement and sponsorship revenue can be provided by expecting concerned government agencies to pay for sponsoring particular programmes. These may be programmes directly meant for helping certain activities; e.g., the health agencies may sponsor programmes on public health education, or family planning; or the agricultural agencies may sponsor general entertainment or other programmes which they consider indirectly important for their mission.

   The External Affairs Ministry may sponsor programmes mainly on the radio (but in the border States even on TV) beamed at foreign audiences.

c. At least for some time to come, each government or authority which sets up a programme corporation should make a general grant available to it. In order to ensure fairness and stability in these grants, decisions on them should be taken by the Planning Commission in the Union Government corporations and by the State Finance Commissions (which will come into being in each State under the Panchayati Raj set-up) for the State corporations. The grants for the corporations set up by local bodies or universities will have to be decided for five-yearly periods in the orders setting up the programme agencies.

To ensure that the decentralised set-up does not lead to unfair practices whether on the commercial or on the programme side, two types of provisions may be thought of. The corporations may be brought under the Unfair Trade Practices provision of the MRTP Act. That will ensure that a quasi-judicial-cum-expert agency will be available when necessary to control unfair practices being indulged in either by advertising agencies or by the corporations. On the programme side, a code of conduct should be laid down in the basic statute regarding the broadcasting set-up, its administration being left to a broadcasting council largely similar to the Press Council.

It is not necessary to lay down greater details about this scheme. My main point in presenting this note is to emphasise that the set-up envisaged in the Prasar Bharati Bill is unlikely to achieve the objectives which are attempted to be attained. A hasty decision on such an important and basic matter will create an unfortunate straitjacket, and it may be years before we can bring about a change. A few more months of countrywide discussion, or examination by a Select Committee of Parliament, should be ensured, before a statute gets finally enacted.

5

Organisational Structure for Autonomous Media

P C Chatterji

I give here a gist of my argument, which I hope to fill in as I go along.

1. I do not believe in the concept of autonomy for the electronic media for India at this stage. It might have been useful forty years ago. Autonomy implies a liberal social order, as existed in Britain when Lord Reith manoeuvred to change the British Broadcasting Company into a public Corporation. Such a polity existed in India in Nehru era. It does not exist in today's polarisation of political parties when no one is prepared to consider a third party as neutral. What we need today is freedom for radio and TV as we have for the Indian Press. What would we ourselves, the participants, the public at large and the Press think of us, if we were to recommend that the Press should function under an autonomous corporation.

2. An autonomous corporation could serve a useful function if it were a short-term measure so that the country could work out the parameters for freedom for radio and TV, which is not synonymous with commercialisation. But I fear that is unlikely. It will take another forty years.

3. Structure is not all important. Much more important is the ethos, the spirit behind the structure. The AIR Code and the directives laid down by Government to the media to present all sides of the picture and to avoid building up personalities should have saved us from the impasse in which we have found ourselves. So long as we, as a people, don't learn to say No, I do not see much hope for the future.

4. Coming now to the structure of the proposed Corporation it is evident that it is the old Prasar Bharati Bill with minor modifications. And the 1979 bill was a watered down version of the Verghese Working group's recommendations. The most important omission was in respect of franchise stations. These stations would have broken the monopoly, though not in respect of news, where the Government's stranglehold most needs to be broken. Here again the present bill shows no forward movement. In the last thirteen years there has been no new thinking.

5. On the Board of Governors I have just two comments to make:

a. I think that there should be one governor who has technical background and is able to provide expert technical advice to the Board. Otherwise the two Engineers-in-Chief, for AIR and DD might feel that they do not have someone in the Board to take up their causes. They would think, and that has been their grouse, that it is the programme personnel who are considered and they are neglected.

b. I oppose the idea that the Chief Executive should be a member of the Board of Governors. The function of the Board should be the framing of policy and keeping a watch over its implementation. Policy is no doubt hard to define, nevertheless, a line of demarcation has to be maintained. Otherwise the Board will continuously be interfering in day-to-day matters. That would be to repeat the situation which exists today, viz., the secretary or rather the joint secretary running AIR and DD from the Ministry!

Incidentally, the importance of the spirit behind the structure is most important at this stage. For instance, will the President appoint independent persons on the Board of Governors? Or, being bound by the Prime Minister's advice, will it be packed with yes-men?

6. The Broadcasting Council is the new name for the Complaints Board of the Verghese Working Group. I am sorry to see that its function is mainly negative. Under clause 14.1 on page 16 of the draft Bill it is stated that the Council "shall receive complaints that a programme or in general, the Corporation, is not functioning in

accordance with the objectives laid down". Again on page 28, in the note on clauses, it is stated that provision is made for the Council to receive complaints. Dr Joshi in his *Report on Doordarshan Software* had assigned a positive function to a similar body. It was to function as a watch dog, especially, in respect of news and current affairs programmes, to ensure that they were objective and balanced. It was further required to see that news personnel were not harassed by the powers that be. I would commend this to the government.

7. In clause 22, relating to instructions to the Corporation by the government, to include in the programmes, or refrain from including, matter which it thinks jeopardises the security of the state, or public order, there is an advance on the 1979 bill. The present bill gives the Corporation the right to announce that it is acting under instructions of the Government. In the earlier bill no such right had been granted. Government had merely stated that it would place a statement on the stable of the House listing the instances in which instructions had been given. But here again the spirit behind the structure comes up. Will the Board of Governors have the courage to put their will against the Government? I have my doubts; as a people we lack the ability to say No.

8. And finally finance. The only source of revenue which AIR and DD have today is a government grant and revenue earned from commercials. The licence fee was abolished years ago and there is little chance of imposing it again. In any case there were too many problems in collecting the fee. Perhaps the public at large is unaware that the Government has, over the last few years, been divesting itself of financial responsibility for a number of services which were provided by Government. These include expenditure on Programme Services, the entire expenditure on commercial services, on training for TV through the Pune Institute and for radio through the Central Institute for Mass Communication, among others. This explains why AIR, and much more so Doordarshan, are at the mercy of advertisers, whose presentations are a daily assault on aesthetic sensibility. Government's statement that it would reduce its financial commitment to the Corporation only means that it will further be at the mercy of commercial interests and consumerism. What price autonomy, and from whom?

6

Developing Infrastructure: A Comment

O P Khushu

THE amount of money involved in the development of broadcasting infrastructure is mind boggling. We have chalked out an VIII plan programme and our present assessment is that it is going to cost us Rs. 8,000 crores over a 5-year period. This includes development of both TV and Radio services. So on an average, the corporation will have to spend over Rs. 1,000 crores per year on some minimal development, the focus of which will really be on consolidation. I say that this is the *minimum* requirement because my feeling is that in popular perception, autonomy does not only mean freedom from government control, it also means, more importantly, excellence. I assume that to the general public, the picture that emerges from all the discussion that has been going on is that we are headed for something that is qualitatively redundant superior to what we have had till now. And if we have to meet that expectation, quite obviously, we will have to provide supporting infrastructural facilities that will enable the corporation to produce programmes of reasonable quality. Now, if you add to this development expenditure the money that would have to be spent merely on running the networks we will require another Rs. 500-600 crores. So the sums of money we are looking at are around Rs. 1,500-2,000 crores a year. Frankly speaking, I don't see that coming from commercial revenue, no matter what we do.

It is generally believed that the money we can drain out from advertising budgets of the corporate sector have, more or less, plateaued. There is very little scope for drawing out more money from the commercial coffers. Perhaps to a small extent, yes, but certainly not to any large extent. Besides, there are other implications, one of them being that this could lead to the creation of new pressure groups. Government is not the only entity that can exercise pressure. Certainly the media can be pressurised by commercial interests. There is a conscious policy on the part of Doordarshan now, to move as quickly as possible away from the concept of sponsorship, to generate more and more programming in-house, employing our own producers or perhaps, by assignment and so on.

One of the suggestions made here concerns the mopping up of the excise duty which is levied on receivers. I do not think that would amount to very much. I will take you back a little in history. Initially we had a licensing system operating within this country, but then this was replaced by a one-time licence levy which was, I don't remember the exact amount, perhaps Rs. 200 or thereabout. This was the sum of money that a buyer paid at the time of purchasing a set. Eventually, this was converted into an addition to the excise duty. Now, assuming that the sum of money you could take away for each set sold was Rs. 200, which is not a very small sum of money in the Indian context, and if you are selling 3 million sets a year, the total money that would accrue from this measure would be in the region of Rs. 60 crores, which is just a drop in the ocean. If we do not provide the corporation the means for selling its services—BBC is a self-sufficient organisation because basically it sells its products which are programme services, by levying licence fees—how will the corporation meets its expenses? Frankly, I don't see the government at any point of time saying that we can revive a licence fee because that will be a very unpopular decision. At any rate, I don't see the seeds of that in the Prasar Bharati Bill or the statements accompanying that Bill. If commercial revenue is the only possible source of funding that we have to look forward to, we can see that there is going to be a wide gap between what we require and what we hope to get. So funding from Government seems to be absolutely inevitable. The possibility of self-sufficiency, in a period of 5 years or 10 years, seems to me to be very, very remote.

The other point I wish to deal with at this stage is about community viewing. Community viewing today is not as popular as it was 10 years ago. There is a great deal of private ownership of sets, people like to watch television in the intimacy of their homes. Community viewing schemes whenever they exist, are operating extremely inefficiently. Many of the sets are poorly maintained, there is no organisation worth its name, there is no management structure that ensures that these sets function properly. Nevertheless, I will give you some figures which will indicate to you the amounts of money that we are talking about. If one were to look at a scenario in which every village had one community viewing set—there are more than 5 lakh villages in India— the amount of money, needed just for buying colour TV sets would be Rs. 500 crores. And you would have to add to this the expenditure on civil works—in many places we would have to provide appropriate shelter—as well as power supply arrangements. The tendency on the part of the government is to declare a village electrified just because there is a single lamp bulb somewhere on the street which is lit. Our experience with the community viewing scheme has been that there are numerous villages which are said to be electrified, but you just cannot find a power socket anywhere. So we will have to provide, in a very large number of these places, solar panels or other alternate sources of energy like a petrol generator. Therefore, a more realistic number would be around Rs. 1,000 crores. Well, who is to make that kind of investment? Whether this country can afford it or not is not something I am qualified to discuss.

The last point I would like to discuss relates to the proposed management structure. I am grateful to Mr Chatterjee for having remembered to mention that engineering should find representation in the Board of Governors. That seems so obvious to all of us. Yet we were startled to find that there was absolutely no provision for it. In fact, even in some of the statements I have seen about the clauses that would possibly see amendment before the Bill is discussed in the Parliament, the proposed structure does not figure at all. I think what Mr Chatterjee said about engineers applies in equal measure to the Directors General who are basically the chief executives of the two organisations. They find no representation in the Board of Governors.

There was a very generous proposal from Mr Paranjape for a separate engineering corporation. This is not the only solution. A formal representation from the AIR and DDI Engineers' Association is that engineering should continue to be a function within the framework of the Government, and the engineering department should be retained by the Government. I am personally opposed to the idea.

First of all, I think it is unworkable. More importantly, I believe that if engineering remains with the Government, it can be used far more effectively than finance as an instrument of control. To give you a very simple example of what could happen, suppose there was something happening that was significant enough for a particular political party to demand its coverage, and if the government of the day wanted to sabotage the decision of the Board of Governors, the simplest thing for it would be to direct the engineer-in-chief to declare the technical facilities unserviceable. (Well, it does happen that at times we are not able to cover a function because an OB van is non-functional). Well then the government could simply tell the engineer-in-chief that if he were to preserve his position, he had better say that the OB van was out of commission even if it actually was not. This may sound bizzare and a very remote possibility, but the point is that engineering can be used as a very effective instrument of control.

Mr Paranjape provides an effective answer to that. He says that the engineering function could be placed with a separate corporation. I ask, why not? That's the model that operates in other areas. You have the National Airport Authority, the IAA which services the international airports. I can see that concept being very closely related to something else he says in his paper: i.e., the concept of multiple corporations. Now if you had several corporations looking after different areas of TV and Radio Broadcasting and they had to be serviced by one single engineering entity, then quite obviously, a separate corporation would be the best solution. I do not, frankly, see the need for a separate engineering corporation servicing another single corporation entirely responsible for programming. That would make good sense only if there were multiple corporations responsible for programme production (let us say, distinct corporations for Radio and TV). If the entire programme activity must reside in a single body, I see considerable merit in keeping the engineering function within a unified corporation as has been proposed in the Bill. However, the positions of authority, the positions of decision-making, must reflect in some way or the other, the relative importance of the roles that various disciplines play. It seems absurd to me that finance, personnel management and recruitment find representation in the Board of Governors, but programme-making and technology do not.

7

Current Affairs Programmes

Harish Khanna

THE current debate on securing autonomy for the Indian electronic media, namely, Akashvani and Doordarshan, has rightly zeroed in on the character of quality of News and Current Affairs, which are most susceptible to the prevalent culture. These programmes do not occupy even 20 per cent of the broadcast time; yet, they have come to be regarded as the true index of the quality of broadcasting as well as a touchstone for genuine autonomy of the professionals, and the tone of the broadcasting organisation as a whole.

The range of current affairs programmes indicate the level of socio-political sensitivity of the broadcasters as well as the limits imposed on content and style. Besides, current affairs programmes give a good indication of the maturity and professional excellence of cadres engaged in planning and producing these programmes.

It is pertinent to recall that the National Front's decision to give high priority to the task of, what has been soulfully described as 'emancipation of the media', arose out of an appreciation of the fact that existing structures and dispensations had often tended to favour the government in power, most of the time against the interest of the opposition.

There had been complaints about the bias in some newspapers and periodicals too especially produced by ambitious journalists who have long abandoned the basic dictum of good journalism that views and news ought to be separated. However, the protest never acquired a desperate tone because multiplicity of newspapers militates against the exclusion of contrary facts and views. On the other hand, the monopolistic situation of radio and television renders them far more vulnerable to the charge of bias. The sheer magnitude of the audience of the electronic media—21 million television sets watched by some 10 crore people and 100 million radio sets reaching a massive listenership of 500 million—underscores the awesome gravity of the consequences of control of the media.

A highly virulent campaign against the misuse of government communication media had preceded the inscription of the item of the autonomy of electronic media on the election manifesto of the Front, and the pronouncement of the intention to move towards dismantling of the coercive aspects of the Official Secrets Act in discharge of their commitment to open government and democracy.

Mr P Upendra, Minister of Information and Broadcasting had stated at the time of introducing the Prasar Bharati Bill, 1989 that government's purpose was to safeguard the citizen's right to be informed freely, truthfully and objectively on all matters of public interest, national or international, and to receive contrasting views, without any opinion or ideology of its own being advocated. He concluded his statement by saying that the Bill he was moving was 'a charter of freedom to give voice to the people of India through the fulfilment of their fundamental freedom of speech and expression as enshrined in Article 19(1) (a) of the Constitution.'

We are witnessing high expectations alternating with scepticism. Considering the fact that the issue of media autonomy and the setting up of independent corporations has been receiving public attention since 1964, when the Chanda Committee recommended institutional changes for promoting creativity in broadcasting, and that India narrowly missed the creation of Prasar Bharati in 1979, apprehensions are understandable. People are asking whether the proposed changes will really enhance the credibility of the public media or whether the declared commitment to non-partisan and impartial presentation of news should be believed. What will be the relationship between the government and the two broadcasting organisations under the revised set-up? Let's take the role of Government first to see whether there will be a fundamental change of approach to the discussion of issues over the media and, above all, how the existing staff will cope with the new situation by asserting their independence and professional commitment.

For programmes in general and News and Current Affairs in particular, Akashvani and Doordarshan have guidelines developed by a Committee of professionals led by the eminent journalist-statesman, G Parthasarthy. Similarly, there is a code to regulate Centre-State relations in the matter of access to radio and television. In abstract merit, these guidelines are unexceptionable. But perceptive observers felt that they were often ignored or conveniently side-stepped to accommodate the wishes of the power elite.

There is a belief that an elected government has an inherent right to project its point of view and that the mandate bestowed by the people, also includes projection of values accepted by the nation. This right, however, is not superior to the rights of the people to know and get the opportunity to make independent judgement on government's actions howsoever buttressed by majority support. All attempts to spell out communication policy proved abortive.

I believe the first senior political leader to whom the question was posed was Sardar Vallabhbhai Patel who, as Information and Broadcasting Minister, asserted that a democratically elected government had the right to have access to public media to promote national consensus on major issues by sharing its thinking with the people. Virtually the same position was taken by successive Ministers of Information and Broadcasting. The standard argument based on aggregation of lines and words devoted to the opposition point of view is too familiar to need any explanation. The issue acquired a larger and more critical dimension when the Nehruvian unity of thought and action was confronted by nascent political pluralism. However, the Sardar and Nehru as well as many great leaders of those time never felt cornered by opposition or tempted to shut out dissent; they met criticism with well-reasoned exposition and, above all, firm conviction. As public opinion pressures built up, their successors were often forced into retreat from this position, illustrating the dictum that a government in fright tends to interfere more, relying more on propaganda and less on advocacy.

Thus, there is no difference of opinion about the role of government in explaining to the people the reasons for its actions or trying to involve the people at large in the governance of the nation through shared information. What was sadly forgotten was the vital fact that this right cannot obliterate the right of the opposition to put across its point of view on issues and happenings, more fundamentally the right of the people to be truthfully informed.

An important related question is the capability of the staff to assume a responsible role of presenting facts and views with utmost objectivity and using the broadcast medium to good effect. The Prasar Bharati Bill visualises the transfer of existing staff to the proposed corporation. At present, the news staff is drawn from the Central Information Service, working under the supervision and direction of a senior functionary, also drawn from the CIS. Before the constitution of this service, the News Division used to be headed by experienced journalists. The Director of News Services has always enjoyed a senior hierarchical status, presently that of Additional Director-General. Then there are editors, correspondents and reporters, employed under different terms and conditions. Current Affairs, however, has been traditionally regarded as a separate and distinct section of programmes, produced by a cadre of regular, established professional programme producers under the supervision of a senior executive. The overall superintendence of the News and Current Affairs is entrusted to the two Directors General in Akashvani and Doordarshan, who report to the Ministry of Information and Broadcasting. Since both departments have been organised as attached offices of the Ministry, the line of command has never been questioned.

Unfortunately, no specialisation has been encouraged in Current Affairs, the assignment being regarded as a primarily production task. For content, there has been an almost total dependence on talent from the Press, and other fields of learning. That, in my opinion, has constituted the principal weakness of the system—the News staff belonging to a general information service and the Current Affairs staff performing a midwifery role. Of course, there have been welcome exceptions and that explains the existence of small valleys of sunshine and a few bare, proud peaks. It must be recorded, however, that professional excellence has been achieved in non-political broadcasts, documentaries, features, etc. Controversy is projected if it does not come into clash with declared state policy except on rare occasions.

But how do these functionaries remain *au fait* with government policy, particularly, in periods of flux? Over the years, some informal consultative and briefing mechanisms have been hammered out, using the principal spokesmen of the government as sources of appreciation. Insofar as Current Affairs Programmes are concerned, they are mostly episodic deriving their justification from the collective perception of the authorities, unless they deal with very general issues and subjects in which case they tend to be cold mutton.

It is interesting to speculate how the staff which displays advanced symptoms of dependency shrouded in anonymity, will rise to the new responsibilities under the corporate structure which, to use the expression once used by Lionel Fielden, is "too much government." In the opinion of the veteran broadcaster and journalist, Chanchal Sarkar, 'injecting spirit and independence into a staff conditioned by years of subservience' will be a Herculean task. "Fashioning a 'fifth estate'", he said, 'out of acquiescent human material will prove formidably difficult'. Similarly, the Minister of Information and Broadcasting, Mr Upendra had observed that 'it is not only a structure that will bring the required independence, impartiality, fairness and excellence; it is the people who direct and run this Corporation and the professionals who alone will be able to do this'.

One is tempted to do a comparison with the state of the Press. In the proposed scheme of things the government is the proprietor, but enjoying far more power than the businessmen-owners. Alluding to some recent disturbing trends, S Sahay said that 'proprietors will be proprietors, and given their interest in other industries their approach is understandable, though not forgivable, but what does one say of journalists ever ready to please those in power—for personal gain, political, professional or material. They tend to forget that readers are getting more and more sophisticated and are keeping a cl ›se watch on their activities, just as the voters have been scrutinising he performance of legislators and the government.

Can't w ; effectively insulate the broadcaster from pressures from above v hich could distort their perspective and ultimately turn sensitive and articulate professionals into mute conformists seeking protective solace in the absence of controversy even mediocrity, which seldom attract flak?

The 1978 Verghese design had envisaged a clear separation between the trusteeship role and the executive function. The Prasar Bharati Bill of 1989, however, fuses the two roles. That would make the change of climate difficult, and also expose the government to the same criticism that was directed against the previous one. Mere change of costume will not alter the basic character of the roles. In this respect the BBC pattern of a Governing Board of trustees and a Board of Management under the Director-General which also includes major departmental representatives including Head of Current Affairs, is far superior and above board. To quote Sahay again, 'the safety of the Press lies in numbers and with over 24,000 newspapers in the country, how many could any government control?' Radio and Television being state monopolies are two giant media with an enormous reach and perhaps the main employers of broadcast talent in the country. Some groups, mainly the independent producers, have, therefore, advocated a parallel network or at least, a substantially increased share for outside producers. Competition, they urge, will be a safeguard of credibility as well as quality.

My association with the encouragement of outside film makers and television producers has led me to accept the merit of encouraging independent producers through sponsored programmes but suspect the insidious privatisation of current affairs, which enhances the vulnerability of the broadcast journalist or producer on account of large financial commitments as well as substantial pecuniary rewards, creating an unhappy situation of the producer either treading the safe path of no controversy or building up one's position by even remaining ready to please those in power and surreptitiously propagate the patron's brief through seemingly independent programmes. With a Trust overseeing the development of radio and television and the employment of the media for advocacy and exposition of different views in the public interest, there are better chances of unprofessional conduct being detected and correctives introduced. Trustee-manager as a concept is incapable of standing up to overt and covert pressures of our times.

It is a valid question to ask whether broadcast media, which are subjected to constant pressure from the authorities or powerful interests and lobbies, be made to adhere to a professional code. Broadcasters everywhere, be it UK or the US or India, are strongly averse to codes because they are seem as indirect means of control and manipulation. If that be the case, can public pressures be built to keep the broadcast journalist on the straight path? Different countries have devised different methods to make the broadcaster accountable. In the proposed scheme of things, the Broadcast Council is supposed to perform an ombudsman function. But will the Council have the requisite power?

Admittedly, a truly objective criterion for judging the performance of electronic media is somewhat difficult on account of the evanescent character of the medium, compared to the Press, which uses the more stable printed word. A television image fades soon after registering instantaneous impact. It is followed by a train of images. It is difficult after some time to recall the exact expression, the precise tonal inflection of the speaker. What is recalled is a generalised impression. Thus even the most glaring distortions are forgotten. Try to recall the fulminations of a Kalpnath Rai or the foul-mouthed report of a K K Tewari. The written word of the Press, on the other hand, can not only be judged critically as it is read and re-read, but it also provides a constant point of reference to determine whether a report was fair and objective or whether vital information had been deliberately underplayed or concealed. Radio and Television broadcasts can be monitored but the important difference is that a fleeting sound-bit or a flickering image is quickly forgotten. That is why television has been called 'the ultimate instrument for forgetting,' inducing 'amnesia, the disorder of the advanced electronic societies.' Therefore, to oversee television, greater caution and vigilance is called for as well as a sound ethical underpinning.

Another element which constitutes a basic infirmity of the medium of television is the compulsive appeal of the visual and the dramatic as opposed to the subtle and substantial. Over the years, supported by new technology, a great deal of reliance is being placed on the power of the picture to tell the story even though its impact is fleeting. Thus an element of triviality enters the presentation of events and happenings and exposition of ideas. Television becomes theatre, an existentialist experience.

The main justification for Current Affairs programme is that people are interested in seeing issues in relation to their lives, whether personal or social. There is a strong desire to understand the relationship of events by seeing them from different points of view. Perceptions and analytical capabilities vary. But the desire to know becomes stronger with knowledge and critical faculties become progressively sharper.

A great deal depends on arrangement of facts and opinions, which introduces an element of choice and selectivity. It is not difficult to recall instances of our fake David Frosts playing a cat and mouse game with their subjects, to prove their cleverness, and also instances of simulating an air of crisis to subdue the critical judgement of the viewers. Commissioned current affairs programmes, which are made to order according to a brief, tend to suffer from this weakness unless strong editorial judgement and accountability moderates deviant behaviour.

Selection and editing also raises much more vital issues of censorship. Some recent judgements, particularly the one delivered by Justice Sujata Manchar of the Bombay High Court have castigated the tendency of public media to excise portions of statements in the name of limits on time or programme exigencies. Our courts are also now engaged in examining the validity or otherwise of pre-censorship in the case of video magazines, which are supposed to be certified as films for public exhibition. Justice Hidayatullah's historic judgement in the K A Abbas case had established socially significant principles relevant to the administration of the Cinematograph Act and are bound to influence judicial thinking on video-journalism and the content of sponsored Current Affairs programmes on Akashvani and Doordarshan.

The golden rule is that a broadcasting organisation has no opinion of its own. It has no position to take or ideology to sell. In other words, its main business is to present different points of view in a manner that the listener or the viewer is assisted in forming his or her own independent judgement on the merits of an argument. This detachment is sometimes eroded by pressures from above. If current affairs programmes of a broadcasting network have to serve the basic purpose of objective dissemination of information and highlighting of issues, concrete steps have to be taken not only to inscribe objectivity as a high principle, but also to train the personnel handling information or producing current affairs programmes to take a really detached view and aim at balance. Professionals know that one-sidedness of presentation is sometimes the result of technical incompetence rather than any deliberate intention to deceive. However, one of the critical pressures on the producer of current affairs comes from the tantalising question: how much of the truth should the people be told and when a particular information should be shared? There is evidence to suggest that the ultra-realistic coverage of violence has led to the de-sensitisation of the viewers, resulting in an attitude of cynicism. The most obvious example is the coverage of the conflict in Beirut. There is also evidence to suggest that dramatic depiction of violent insurgency tends to boost the ego of the law-breakers and terrifies the innocent people. Television can turn into political intervention unless professional discipline is exercised. However, suppression of the factual in the coverage of law and order may generate dangerous euphoria which is followed by anger and frustration when the truth dawns. It is ultimately a question of professional judgement on the part of the broadcast journalist to decide what to include and what to keep out.

To sum up, we stand at the threshold of a truly exciting era of socially significant radio and television, which will call upon the creative ingenuity of the professionals and the democratic commitment of the political system. The object of this analytical critique is not to create doubts about the possibilities, but to warn against booby-traps which might frustrate the search for excellence in autonomous media structures and weaken the will to be independent and answerable to the people.

8

Reporting For Electronic Media

K K Sud

HAVING worked in the News Services Division of AIR in different capacities for 25 years from 1956 to 1981, I have been closely connected with important political coverages during this period and have gone through the problems of a radio reporter through various phases, the Nehru era, the brief tenure of Lal Bahadur Shastri with Indira Gandhi as Minister for Information and Broadcasting and later Indira Gandhi's long tenure as Prime Minister. I covered the 1962 war with China, Pakistan's infiltration in Kashmir in 1965 and the capture of Haji Pur by Indian troops, communal riots, the Congress split in 1969, Janata rule and the return of Mrs Gandhi to power in 1980.

The main problem of a radio or TV reporter is that he or she is generally not allowed to function freely in a professional manner. Both civil servants and political rulers want to manipulate the electronic media to serve their own political interests. They do not want radio and TV to cover anything unpleasant, which shows the authority in poor light. This leads to loss of credibility of the electronic media.

Unlike reporters of the press, who are allowed a margin of error in the interest of going in for exclusive stories, reporters of the electronic media cannot afford to go wrong. Hence they play safe and their coverage becomes dull and hand-out based.

Apart from speedy and accuracy, an important requirement in covering political controversies is balance. It is here that a reporter of the electronic media runs into serious difficulties. He is rarely allowed to function in a free and fair manner. The stories are revised, rewritten, cut, killed or replaced at the instance of important persons in the Prime Minister's office or the Ministry of Information and Broadcasting. It is this sort of blatant interference in the functioning of the electronic media that has led to the demand for autonomy for radio and TV.

This interference varies depending on the position of the Government. If a Government is stable, the interference goes down, if its position is shaky, the interference very much increases.

It is therefore essential that all important political parties must agree that like the judiciary and the Election Commission, the electronic media will be allowed to function freely, whichever party may be in power. The ruling party should not expect the electronic media to fight its political battles. It is this sort of understanding among the major political parties in the U.K which has allowed the BBC to function in an objective and independent manner.

What is required is not the so-called functional autonomy but full-fledged autonomy. Government even in the early eighties had declared in Parliament that functional autonomy had already been given to the professionals while in reality there was interference in the work of the professionals at every step. The Chairman and the Board of Governors of the proposed Corporation must provide the cushion for the editors, reporters and producers to work in a free and creative atmosphere.

Whatever the set-up, ultimately AIR and Doordarshan will be judged by the level and performance of their professionals. In the past AIR used to attract talented persons from the field of music, drama, poetry and journalism. Later the trend was reversed and many people went back from the Government to newspapers and news agencies to work as columnists and editors. We should again create conditions in which AIR and Doordarshan attract the best people from these fields.

During my stay in AIR on several occasions I found that if we were clear in our minds that something which we were being asked to do was wrong, we were able to bring round our bosses, official or political, to our point of view or even correct the Government. A classic case was when AIR contradicted, on the basis of a report from its own correspondent in Bombay in 1979, the wrong news given in Parliament by the then Prime Minister, Mr. Morarji Desai, of the death of Jaya Prakash Narayan.

There has been a strong feeling among the staff that the authorities are willing to give greater functional autonomy to private producers in the production of programmes than to their own staff. This is very demoralising for the staff and should not happen.

In 1982 the Media Advisory Committee headed by Mr G Parthasarathy produced excellent guidelines for the broadcast media. These were placed before Parliament and sent to AIR and Doordarshan. It appears the Government was never serious about implementing them. I feel if these had been implemented, there would not have been such an outcry against the electronic media. The new Corporation would do well to look at these guidelines and reissue them to its staff for their guidance.

The Prasar Bharati Bill makes the proposed Corporation accountable to Parliament. One hopes this will not lead to day-to-day interference by individual MPs in the functioning of the Corporation.

9

Practical Aspects of Media Autonomy: Producer's View

Harsaran Pandey

THERE has been a debate raging in the country on the issue of autonomy for the Government electronic media. In the sound and the fury of the debate, it is not clear what the real objectives are. The "rational" lobby assumes that all clear-headed national-minded people do want autonomy, and that it is only the political leaders who are not prepared to let go of the power that comes from total control of radio and television. The public at large has a sneaking suspicion that the government won't really let go of the media despite their professions to the contrary.

There have been dissenting voices from within the two organisations. The engineers have voiced their "nay" to autonomy, as with the formation of a Corporation they see a narrowing of job and promotion avenues, which they today enjoy as a cross-sectoral cadre. Some among the executive cadre of administrators have also expressed concern with at autonomy move.

Let me take the example of Doordarshan, DD for short, as I know its working.

DD has three main cadres or service functions: (a) The production or the creative cadre that actually conceive and produce programmes by which TV is judged, (b) the engineering cadre which runs the entire hardware that brings the programme to the home TV set and (c) the executive cadre who are the managers, and servicing all three are the administrative services. Unless there is a strong, logical connecting link among all the cadres, as there is in the best run TV organisations in the world, something goes wrong with the chain of command and it results in confusion behind the scene, which is visible on the screen.

To understand *why* television programmes are what they are today, we need to understand these structures better. It may be asked: what has this to do with the autonomy question? A lot in fact. The existing structures within DD are antiquated, and unless the winds of change that autonomy promises, go deep within, the fear of the TV professionals is that the change will only be superficial. If DD is to have real autonomy, it must be freed from its internal shackles as well.

However as one listens to intelligent people, from outside the electronic media, one fears they lack knowledge of what happens within DD. Somehow, they have a feeling that DD programmes are bad, because the professionals are either ill-trained, or careless or are not professional; that the fault lies in these persons and not in their situation. As a generalisation this is far from the truth.

The heart of any television organisation is its production cadre, its producers, assistant producers, script writers, scenic designers, cameramen, recordists, musicians, performers and so on. In professionally run TV organisations, all structures revolve around them, to service their needs. The biggest investment of a TV station is in this pool of manpower; it is crucial that great care is taken in selecting the best, training them, and giving them the tools and the freedom to produce good programmes. The management hierarchy is from *among* them, and all planning and programming, and programme scheduling has their total involvement. This is the profile of a good TV set-up.

But this is not true with DD. Here the production cadre has been placed right at the bottom of a long line of executives, station directors, deputy directors, assistant directors and so on. The methodology of control is normally for the bureaucrat to receive his instructions from the Ministry or the Directorate, and these are passed on to a hapless producer who is expected to fall in line and somehow, using his/her ingenuity gather the basic wherewithal to produce a programme. Not every programme is made like this, of course, but this happens often enough to upset the entire system. And this is true not only of Current Affairs programmes, but also of more innocuous ones. A fertiliser week or some anniversary is suddenly made to be inserted in the schedule.

The problem with this methodology is that even at the start of such an exercise, the producer begins with the demoralising certainty that the best programme in the circumstances will be a mediocre one. Why? Because most "Command performance" programmes have to be done in a hurry. The producer has no reference library that can support him, he has little by way of archives for retrieval of footage and has to fight other equally tense producers, scrabbling for limited facilities, for preview, filming, editing, voicing, etc. I will elaborate this point later.

Producers do prepare programme schedules for three months for their programmes, and do decide on some programme content, but the in-house interaction, between bosses and producers is an unhappy one—the producers buffeted about—the bosses harassed from further up to achieve the impossible.

It is essential that the executive cadre should not be divorced from the production cadres. Recently producers have been promoted to executive posts, but it is essential that this does not tie them down to desks—but instead their experience is used for bringing better insights to programme making.

A more coherent grouping of programmes is needed and each head should be led by a Chief Producer, e.g., Entertainment, Documentaries, Drama, Music, Dance, Talk shows, Sports, News and Current Affairs, etc. Here is an example:

Chief Producer (Entertainment) (in-charge of budget, annual planning of programmes)

Dy. Chief Producer (Drama) ---------- Dy Chief Producer Music

Senior Producer (Drama)

Producers

While the Chief Producer would plan the schedule for the years, on budget, thrust, types of programmes, the specific entertainment producer, (e.g. Drama) would concentrate on his or her area, and under him the specific features allotted to them.

Today the chief and the other executives are more involved in monitoring the performance of the producer than in planning the programmes. If the entire team plans, there is coherence of approach, if the top executive is one who has reached that position after years of having been a production person himself, he knows the media. Executive officers who may have been promoted from AIR, or other field services, or who have little production experience, or who may be transferred between Drama and Sports (or other programmes), can do little to help the programme. And yet, at the same time they may create an additional bottleneck for the producer struggling to get his product out.

Another area of concern is facilities. These have never been able to keep up with the growing needs of DD. In the early 1970's with the first expansion of Doordarshan there was time to select personnel carefully, who were fully trained before they actually entered a station. There was time for innovation and experiment. But suddenly more stations came on stream and you could feel the fabric of infrastructure stretch. We were assured that this would change. This was true of trained personnel, equipment and space. Producers stood nervously and tense in queues for cameras, for editing and studio space, anxiously fighting other producers who also had programmes unfinished, and scheduled for the same day. From here to the 'one LPT a day' era, the government settled for the criteria of quantity rather than quality and the onus of getting the programme out remains with the producer.

A new autonomous structure must also ensure a totally new structure within. Those commanding and those executing must be part of the same team, discussing, debating, even dissenting, for the cause of better programming. The producers will have to be restored to their position as leaders of the team, as prescribed by every television training school and manual. Unless these norms are set right, all DD will remain as new. The staff must have greater mobility; space must be provided for a full, up-to-date research and reference system. Until new studios are made space must be count or hired. Doordarshan can no longer live out of a suitcase like a travelling salesman.

New talent has grown in the country, outside the DD system—the good among them must be encouraged, but the bad, those totally without qualification must be weeded out.

Somewhere along the way to the top in the numbers game, Doordarshan lost its soul as its own people became demoralised. Without being given the tools for professional output, they were ridiculed and held in contempt in comparison with "daring" programmes by private producers or worse, compared to BBC production.

Doordarshan has a professional cadre. It is time to get the right perspective on where they should stand. Until and unless they—who make the programmes—begin to matter, Doordarshan cannot regain its soul, autonomy or no autonomy.

10

Technical Feasibility and Cost of Decentralised TV and Radio

O P Khushu

BEFORE I examine, in any manner of depth, the viability and economics of establishing alternate programme channels, I think it would be in order to give you a summary of where we stand today with respect to the first TV channel.

As you are aware, there has been a phenomenal growth in television coverage in recent years. In fact, television in the true sense was born in India in 1984. We had a modicum of television operating in the country till that time, but no one could have imagined in 1982, that in just 8 years from then we would be in the state that we now find ourselves in. This has had its positive as well as negative aspects, but we could discuss that a little later. Today the Doordarshan network consists of something like 479 transmitters, the bulk of which are low power transmitters (LPT), meaning those with power outputs of 100 watts or less. Out of these 479 transmitters, the high power ones are only 55 which will increase to 84 after the completion of on-going schemes. In terms of coverage, we today claim to provide signal to something like 76 per cent of the country's population which is contained in only 54.5 per cent of the area of the country. In other words, half the country in a physical sense is still not covered. And I might add that when we say 76 per cent of the population is served by television, we are telling only a half truth. This number includes the population in the fringe areas where people must use very tall antennas and in several cases, also boosters to be able to obtain satisfactory reception.

Upon completion of the on-going schemes, which will mean setting up of another 30 odd high power transmitters which are in various stages of implementation, (we will probably complete the programme in the next year or year-and-a-half), the population coverage will increase to 84 per cent and the area coverage to 69.6 per cent. But if we apply the more stringent international standards which determine the usefulness of a service, then the actual population coverage will be no more than about 60 per cent. This is startling, as it is generally believed that TV is now available throughout the country.

Now let us look at what it would cost us to increase the coverage from 60 per cent, reckoned against international standards, to a figure as close to 100 per cent as possible. 95 per cent is a good figure. Generally, the residual 5 per cent would not be served even in the best of conditions. I might mention the case of Japan, for instance, where they have 7,000 transmitters of various power levels operating in the country, but there is a certain percentage of its population which is not yet covered.

To increase the coverage from 60 per cent to 95 per cent, we will need to add something like 140 high power transmitters plus another 500 gap fillers in the form of low power transmitters and transposers. According to an estimate we framed a year-and-a-half ago, which needs to be updated, the cost of setting up these additional transmitters would be in the range of Rs. 1,275 crores to Rs. 1,800 crores.

The present network of transmitters is supported by 18 programme production centres which have been in operation for quite a while now. The number next year is likely to rise to 48 after the on-going projects are completed. Several of these remaining 30 programme production centres have been completed, but we have not commissioned them basically because we have an acute shortage of staff, particularly in the cadres of producers and production assistants. We also have a very large fleet of field production facilities (Outside Broadcast Vans and EFP Vans—roughly 23 of them which have given us a great deal of mobility).

We have a vast network of TVRO terminals which work with the INSAT satellites for the purpose of receiving satellite delivered programmes for rebroadcast purposes. We also operate a full-fledged teletext service, presently only in Delhi but hopefully, we will be able to extend it to Bombay shortly and Madras and Calcutta a little later.

The backbone of the system at the present time is this very large network of low power transmitters (LPTs). We chose this model very appropriately in the early '80s because this met three basic requirements which had been set for the expansion programme at that time. The first was that we must be able to implement the expansion programme in the quickest possible time. It was also laid down that equipment must be obtained from indigenous sources and most importantly, we had to be able to locate these transmitters in areas of high population density so that we could have maximum yield by way of population coverage in the quickest possible time. This model served us very well because at that point of time, investing Rs. 30-35 lakhs in an LPT enabled us to cover a city, let us say as large as Aligarh with a population of over 5 lakhs. Today this model of expansion has become inapplicable and unremunerative for the simple reason that we have covered all towns with a population in excess of 50,000. Every new LPT that we set up now will not serve a very large population. The big problem with this LPT model of expansion has been that we have consumed our frequencies very rapidly and we already have had to move over to the Ultra High Frequency (UHF) band. The VHF bands I and III have been more or less exhausted. So this approach has been inefficient from the frequency utilisation point of view.

This LPT model of expansion has led to the creation of a network which is Delhi-centric. We have a national programme which is satellited and received at various locations and rediffused using terrestrial transmitters. There is no local programme injection except at the 18 programme production centres which I mentioned previously. But this has been only the very first step forward in our movement towards the ultimate objective, which has been declared as a 3-tier broadcasting structure with distinct elements of national, regional and local services. Parallel with this development of a national service, we have now also introduced regional services. We have satellite-based regional services operating in 3 states—Andhra Pradesh, Maharashtra and Tamil Nadu—where the programmes produced at the capital centres are uplinked to the satellite, received back at all the transmitting centres in the states concerned and re-broadcast.

We have also established similar regional services in 3 other states, i.e., West Bengal, Kerala and Punjab but in these states, we use the terrestrial microwave network, not the satellite.

Our emphasis on expansion of the national service has been

viewed adversely by some media critics. In fact, in the morning, Dr Rao made a forceful plea that if we cannot link up the LPTs with local or state programme production centres, these might just as well be closed down. He asked whether there was a way by which this could be done. Well, the easiest way, of course, is to send a team of people with sledge hammers to break them!

Personally I feel that the concept along which we proceeded was sound. We were going in the right direction, but somewhere along the way, the national service came to be confused with a Delhi originated service. This was not the concept. The national service was expected to be composed of programme contributions from the regional centres. It was basically an assembly function that was to take place at Delhi. This was certainly not conceived as a Delhi-based service. But one tends to take soft options. Because of various constraints, both in terms of the manpower, financial resources and so on, that concept could not be realised. I must admit that in today's context, the national service does tend to be an extension of the Doordarshan Kendra at Delhi. However, we have wilfully moved on to the development of the regional services (the second tier of the eventual structure), and these already operate in 5 states.

Hopefully, when adequate satellite capacities become available (we have had major setbacks in the INSAT system), we should be able to extend this regional services to all other states. Then the worry we all have about LPT's carrying programme services that are irrelevant need not to exist. I think that kind of a situation will develop in the course of the next few years. If our own satellite programme does not move forward as planned, we will still have the lease option and we should be able to obtain additional capacities.

This is where we stand at present. The question specifically posed to me is about the second channel. We see the second channel as the third level of the proposed 3-tiered structure, which is the local service. As you are aware, we have a second channel already operating in the 4 metropolitan cities—Delhi, Bombay, Calcutta and Madras. We have proposed the establishment of the second channel in 16 other places, all state capitals except the smallest ones.

Is it possible to establish a second channel, purely from the point of view of technology? The answer, quite clearly, is yes, but let us see how that can be done. The simplest way, of course, is to develop additional networks of transmitters. We have a network of transmitters servicing the first channel. We need, more or less, a similar number of transmitters to service the second channel. We did a rough exercise, again a-year-and-a-half ago, and we came to the conclusion that if he have to build a second channel providing an aggregate of 95 per cent coverage of the country, then we will need to establish something like 220 high power transmitters and 729 LPTs and transposers. On the basis of the price prevailing at that time, we estimated that this would cost us something like Rs. 2,000 crores. I am sure this figure will need to be substantially enhanced if we have to take into account the cost escalation which has taken place since then. One can see quite easily that this is an extremely expensive proposition. As I mentioned earlier, if we have to increase the coverage of the first channel to 95 per cent, we will need to invest a minimum of Rs. 1,275 crores. And in addition to that, would have to pump into the system something like Rs. 2,000 crores to be able to create a second channel.

This is just the cost of transmitters. It does not include programme production costs. I might add that there have been demands for a third channel for specific programme services like distance-education, support to open universities and so on. In fact, a specialist group was created by the Ministry of Human Resources Development to look into that aspect. It came up with a report that said a dedicated set of transmitters would be needed because if televison is to be used in support of distance education, one needs to find time which is suited to the student community. Now, by definition, an open university student is one who works. So the only time he is free is in the evening, and that is precisely the time which is regarded as the peak viewing time for the normal Doordarshan programmes. The group assessed that the dedicated channel would have to work for 18 hours a day supporting only education, agricultural extension and other similar services. So, if one had to establish this third channel, an additional sum of about Rs. 2,000 crores would have to be invested.

Money is not the only problem. An even bigger problem is the limitation of available space in the radio frequency spectrum. As I said earlier, we have consumed Band I in the VHF range, and more or less consumed Band III as well. We have moved on to the UHF range of frequencies. We met with some resistance initially because this meant that people had to buy different antennas, and in certain cases, additional tuners to be fitted to the old black and white sets which had only single channel capability. But now, by and large, viewers have got used to the change, channel converters are now inexpensive, and UHF antennas are available. So, UHF is being accepted by the general public.

Frequencies are allocated by the International Telecommunications Union (ITU) through a process of Administrative Radio Conferences. There is enough room in the frequency allocations made by the ITU for several television channels, in every country. But it is not obligatory on the part of the administrations to follow the table of frequency allocations laid down by the ITU. They can make changes subject to the condition that these do not adversely affect the operation of radio communication systems in other countries.

When the Indian administration, which is represented in the ITU by the Wireless Planning and Coordination wing of the Ministry of Communications, looked at the totality of requirements projected by various radio communication users in the country, they developed what is called a National Frequency Allocation Plan. In this Plan, we find that the number of channels, the total spectrum space available to television broadcasting, is considerably less than the space allocated to this service in the table of frequency allocations laid down by ITU. If one were to restrict the use of frequencies to what has been allocated in the National Frequency Allocation Plan, I am afraid there is not enough room to support even a second channel, leave alone a third.

There is a very strong case for opening up more and more frequency channels to television broadcasting. We have initiated some action in this direction. This again has to go through an inter-departmental consultation process and I am hoping that over a period of time, we will be able to get access to the entire spectrum that the ITU has allocated to Broadcasting service. If that happens, there will be enough frequencies available in the allocated spectrum to support 3 channels of television.

This is not the only scenario. One might give up and say that if it is going to cost Rs. 2,000 crores just to develop an alternate channel of transmission, which is an exorbitant sum of money, would it mean that we would never get towards a second channel? As I indicated earlier, we are already making a beginning. In the draft VIII Plan, we have a proposal for 16 second channel transmitters at a cost of Rs. 630 crores, which is roughly Rs. 40 crores a piece. This includes not just the cost of transmitters, but also the cost of the complementary programme production facility.

There are other possible scenarios. One is the satellite scenario. I am referring to the concept of direct broadcasting satellites (DBS). Way back in 1987, there was an initiative on the part of the ITU to develop a plan for the operation of broadcasting satellites in the geostationary orbit which would operate in what is called the Ku Band. This is a band that makes it possible to have satellite transmissions which can provide signals receivable with a small, inexpensive receiver.

Such a receiver is called an individual receiver and sometimes simply a home receiver. It generally means a TV set together with an additional piece of equipment than can be retrofitted, and a small antenna--about 60 cms to 75 cms in diameter. At that time the expectation was that if such receivers were to be produced in bulk, at the rate of about a million sets a year, then the additionality in cost over an ordinary TV set would perhaps be of the order of 50 US dollars, which was not much. Mind you, at that time a dollar was equivalent to only ten rupees. We thought that this was a very attractive proposition and we ought to implement it to whatever extent possible.

We submitted our requirements to the ITU projecting that we would need to set up a satellite facility that would provide 4 TV channels in the Ku band. Incidentally, in the Ku band, beams coming out from the satellite are very narrow and one cannot cover an area very much larger than, say, a state or perhaps, two adjoining states. That, in my opinion, is a very attractive feature of this particular band, because you can tailor programming to the area served. We said we would eventually have to aim at something like 4 TV channels in each state, or a combination of two states. In order to cover the whole of India, we sought frequency allocations in orbital positions for 12 beams emanating from a satellite or a set of satellites, each beam supporting 4 TV channels. So that made 48 TV channels in all, 4 of them in each of the 12 beams. We managed to get the orbital slots and also the frequencies, but then we were not able to implement the proposed system because, at that time, the value of satellite-backed TV services had not become evident to the policy makers.

Following the Satellite Instructional Television Experiment (SITE) which was conducted in India in 1975-76 and subsequently, the STEP experiment which was carried out with the help of a

Franco-German satellite, the Department of Space had begun to look at the possibilities of launching a series of satellites and came up with the concept of a multiple-purpose satellite network catering to the requirements of broadcasting, telecommunications as well as weather prediction. Today it seems surprising that at that point of time, when the report offered by the DOS was examined by the Cabinet, investment on the space segment was approved, but that on the TV ground segment was not approved.

The government did not see the relevance of a satellite system to TV at that time (today the TV component happens to be the core of the INSAT system). The need had not become evident then, so one could not suggest a massive investment in broadcasting satellites. However, eventually the INSAT system was approved in totality and it is common knowledge that this radically transformed the TV situation in the country.

We have begun to look seriously at DBS to provide an alternate programme option to viewers. In terms of capital cost, it is a fairly inexpensive proposition. I have some figures which illustrate this. A satellite of the INSAT-II class would cost us roughly, inclusive of launch charges, Rs. 220 crores. It is not good engineering practice to have only one satellite supporting a vital service like TV. We need to have at least two. Experience has shown to us that we should preferably have three. (We had a series of failures in the INSAT system. We have felt very insecure at times and the main reason why the TV service has survived till today is that we exercised some timely lease options on Arabsat and Statsionar systems. We have no INSAT satellite which is effectively usable today, INSAT I-B being in the limping phase at the moment.) If we had two satellites in orbit, one as the main functional satellite and the other as a back-up, the system would cost us about Rs. 400 crores.

The problem here is that between those 2 satellites, we would not be able to realise all of the 48 channels. I mentioned previously because these will carry high power transponders which consume very high energy. Let me mention here that it is generally assumed that a telecommunication satellite is similar to a direct broadcast satellite. It is not. In fact, there is a basic difference: in the case of a telecom satellite, we put all the complexity in the ground segment, which means that we establish a very large earth station, let us say with an 11 mt antenna, receiving signals from low-power transponders in space. We get a very feeble signal, but then, we are able to receive it because we have a large ground station.

In the case of a broadcasting satellite, it is necessary to reverse this complexity. This means that we put most of the available resources in the space segment, obtain a strong signal so that we can have a very simple, inexpensive terminal on the ground for reception. Therefore, DBS transponders are high-power transponders which consume a lot more energy. If we take into account the limitation that arises from the total power that can be generated on a spacecraft, we cannot accommodate more than about six transponders in a spacecraft of medium size, such as an INSAT satellite.

If you have two DBS satellites, we can perhaps have altogether 12 channels, which means we would be able to provide one TV channel in each of the 12 beams I mentioned. In other words with an investment of Rs. 400 crores, we can provide a second channel available throughout the country.

The problem really is not the cost of the satellites. The main problem is the cost of consumption of the service. It is alright for us to say that a satellite or a series of satellites is covering the whole country, but it does not follow that nothing need be done for further development of the terrestrial network. The fact of the matter is that a viewer has to invest more money in a DBS receiver. I do not think we are going to get anywhere near a production level of one million sets a year that I mentioned previously. At the production levels that one can realistically expect to achieve, we should be prepared to accept that a satellite receiver, or the additionality to a colour TV set in order to be able to receive a TV signal, will be expensive. A colour TV set with necessary add-ons to be able to receive satellite signal would easily cost at least twice as much as an ordinary set.

The question is: given the high cost of consumption, is DBS relevant in the Indian context? I must confess that we do not have the answer at the present moment. We do not know whether DBS is the right way to go.

We know, of course, that it may be the right way to go for certain kinds of services, such as value added services not addressed to the common man, services for which some people are willing to pay (one might perhaps use scrambling to ensure access only to those who subscribe). Some of the value-added services one could consider are High Definition Television (HDTV) and some of the international services, which could be re-broadcast from these satellites, such as

Murdoch's Sky channel. For such services, DBS is, in my opinion, a better alternative, because it is less expensive than a parallel network of terrestrial transmitters and provides a one shot service instantly, but developing a terrestrial network of transmitters is a tardy process requiring years to accomplish. The negative aspect of course, is the higher cost of consumption. I am hoping for the day when the cost of DBS receivers comes down to within the reach of the common man. I do not think that the day is far off. I might add that when S Band direct reception sets produced by companies like Shyam Antenna, were first introduced in the market for INSAT reception, one talked of a price level of seventeen to eighteen thousand rupees for a suitable add-on to a colour TV cost. The same equipment now costs around eight thousand rupees. Thus, inflation notwithstanding, the prices have come down to half. I am hoping that there will be a breakthrough in technology and it will be possible to market these receivers even more cheaply. This is the reason why I am personally not very enthusiastic about investing our capital money in establishing a terrestrial network of transmitters for the second channel, apart from the 16 that I mentioned previously. My belief being that in another 4-5 years the whole scenario is likely to change and the satellite option will become far more viable.

The third possibility is cable TV. I might say that cable TV is now more real in India than most of us imagine. Networks have begun to proliferate and I know of some which have more than 2,000-3,000 subscribers. The only reason why they have not grown even further is that there is a certain degree of ambiguity in the perception of the related law. One doesn't know whether this activity is legal or illegal; I might add, even the government does not seem to know. There are provisions in the Indian Telegraph Act that some people claim are violated, but others do not agree. The government has woken up to this uncertainty and an inter-departmental group has been set up to look into the whole matter. Hopefully, in the next few months, this group will make an appropriate recommendation to the government. But it is important to recognise that cable TV has already become a reality in this country and it is serving a very large number of people.

What does it take to establish a cable TV network? I have done a few calculations for some typical scenarios. Assume, for instance, that one were to establish a network in a metropolitan city like Delhi with a subscriber density of something like 5,000 in a cell of 1 km x 1 km. If we take into account the cost of the trunk line, the distribution amplifiers, splitters, and everything else that is needed, it turns out that the investment per subscriber is only about Rs. 1,000, which I do not believe is very expensive, considering that a good TV antenna today costs Rs. 300-400.

If one considered a village or a small town situation, one would not expect more than 100 subscribers in this typical cell of 1 km x 1 km. The investment here would be of the order of Rs. 2,500 per subscriber. Again, not a large sum of money, especially in an area where the DDI network does not yet reach.

This is the initial capital investment. The recurring expenditure will depend on the cable operator, and the software offered by the cable network. In Thailand, people pay something like 100 US dollars for an initial connection, and a monthly charge of about 25 US dollars.

If the cable operator decides to put into the network a public service television channel (a DDI programme), the VCR playback of a bought out programme and an international satellite channel (for example, CNN), his investment will not be very large. But, on the other hand, if he produces programmes specially for the cable network, his investment will have to be very large and the amount of subscription that people will have to pay will increase correspondingly. This is why I am not considering a typical scenario in relation to recurring costs.

Despite relatively insignificant costs, many people think that cable TV is relevant to the Western societies, but not to India. I do not claim to have an understanding as to whether or not cable TV is the right thing in our country. Social scientists know better. But, may I point out that you may take a view on cable TV, decide it is offensive to public interest and as a consequence take appropriate regulatory measures, but what can you do about signals coming from across the borders, especially through satellites? Soon American programmes will begin to be seen in India. Right now you can pick up CNN being transmitted 24 hours a day through a hired transponder on one of the Russian satellites. Chinese signals are being received in India. I know of several Intelsat signals which are receivable in India carrying different programmes from time to time (Intelsat is a commercial system).

Something even more startling has happened recently. A satellite retrieved from space after a mislaunch has been acquired by a Hong Kong based company (a consortium that includes Chinese and

British investors) and successfully launched. It was a copy book launch, absolutely flawless, and the satellite (called Asiasat) will be operationalised in a month's time. We are ourselves negotiating a lease arrangement with Asiasat for a few transponders. Nineteen of the 24 transponders have already been sold out. What is not widely known is that a few of these transponders have been bought by a private production company which obviously has a cable TV as well as a DBS interest in this part of the world.

So, sooner or later we are going to have access to programmes, perhaps tailor-made for sub-continental audiences, transmitted by external sources which will be available throughout India.

Time has come for us to be able to monitor and see what signals are coming in. We have made a proposal in the VIII Plan document for establishing a monitoring centre with antenna that can be pointed to any orbital position in the visible arc.

11

Educational TV

B N Koul

THAT the organisers of the seminar on "Autonomy and After: Government Media" have shown their concern about educational TV by inviting an academic to participate in the deliberations is a gesture of immense satisfaction to me personally. This is so essentially because educational TV is still almost a non-concern for the Government media in this country. I should immediately add that I am aware of the UGC Programmes being telecast by Doordarshan and also various Science Quiz Programmes that have been appreciated by the masses all over the country. Besides, there are many programmes in the form of serials and those in the area of agriculture etc., which impart education of one or the other type to people who may show their interest in them. But we need to make a distinction between educative TV and educational TV. Depending on who the receiver is, almost any programme will show a few features of educative TV, for example, by watching serials on wild life, we learn about animal behaviour, environment and ecology, and similarly, from serials like Mahabharat, we learn about human nature, socio-political conflicts, different values, history, etc. All this is educative TV, and the media in India provides a reasonable amount of such TV. But educational TV, as I said above, is still a thing of the future in our country. While saying so, what is in my mind is something like Channel No. 8 of Houston TV in Texas (USA). All the programmes on this channel have clear-cut educational objectives and the production and presentation are all geared to achieve those educational objectives. We have very little of this type of educational TV available in this country today.

While talking about 'autonomy' with respect to education one is inclined to think of two types: (i) autonomy of the institution, and (ii) autonomy of the clientele.

In all probability, and I am certain about it, most of the participants of the seminar will remain concerned with the former, i.e., the institutional autonomy—matters pertaining to the organisational structure of Doordarshan, role of producers, handling of current affairs and entertainment programmes, technical feasibility and cost effectiveness of multi-channel transmission vis-a-vis the autonomy proposed in Prasar Bharati Bill.

As for the latter, i.e., autonomy of the clientele, very little will be said and much less discussed as the notion is relatively new. For educational TV, the clientele consists of the students who use TV as an educational medium; by the autonomy of the student we mean that stage of educational affairs in which students can decide on the objectives of the education which they are looking for, decide on the pedagogical methods and materials they would like to use to achieve those objectives and also decide on the type of evaluation to establish whether the educational objectives they set before themselves have been achieved or not.

I am bringing in this notion of 'learner autonomy' partly because my concern is open and distance education, the ultimate objective of which is 'learner autonomy', and partly because I hope that autonomous Doordarshan will be not only 'sensitive' to the educational needs of the people of this country, but also be aware of its own potential as a significant educatior. Thus, besides generating sufficient will to fulfil its responsibilities as an educator of immense strength, it will play a key role in building a society of 'autonomous learners'.

This is, seemingly, an unattainable objective. Autonomous Doordarshan cannot even reflect on this objective unless it becomes aware of both the rudimentary and the complex problems involved in planning, developing, producing and implementing/presenting educational programmes. Our media lack this awareness at present, as has already been pointed out.

It is with this view-point that I think it advisable to talk about some of our experiences with media, especially when used for educational purposes.

1. We (at Indira Gandhi National Open University) have learnt that an otherwise experienced and technically sound producer cannot necessarily be a good educational TV producer. Initially when we

started preparing our video and audio programmes it was felt that if the topic was given to the producer, he/she would produce the relevant video/audio on his/her own. It was before long that this practice had to be given up in favour of giving an academic brief to the producer to work on. 'Academic brief' is a page (or so) long note saying who the programme is addressed to, what its theme is, what is its length, how it may begin, what discussion points may it touch upon, what its focus may be, etc. Sometime later it was felt that in addition to the academic brief an elaboration to the academic brief known as an 'academic note' also was needed—this note it was suggested could be 8-10 pages long, making suggestions about visuals besides incorporating the essential text expected to be presented. Still later, it was realised that constant discussion, interaction and exchange of ideas between the academic and producer was not only desirable but also essential in order to produce a pedagogically effective media unit. The conflict was something like this:

i. the producer thought that he/she was the right person to produce the audio/video and he/she was qualified to do so. On the other hand, the academic thought that he/she was the right person to do so, for he/she was the master of the discipline being presented through the audio/video programme. It is obvious that to produce an effective educational programme the producer has to be an academic also, or, the other way round, the academic has to be the producer too. It is, therefore, not without reason that the BBC/UKOU (British Broadcasting Corporation/United Kingdom Open University) usually appoint as producers the academics trained in audio/video production.

ii. secondly, it has been observed that an average producer pays greater attention to the 'frame' and how the spaces in the 'frame' are filled properly and adequately, besides being inclined to give an 'entertaining' slant to the programme. The academic on the other hand, remains concerned with the 'content', i.e., the message he wants to convey to the student. It may be for similar reasons that a producer remains concerned with the presentability of the presenter and other faces and their voices while the academic would like to get the message conveyed by a person who can talk about and/or present the themes with understanding and authority.

A simple lesson from this experience is that we have yet to make a beginning in the area of educational TV. The case of producer-academic conflict is a mere example; the point to be made is that educational TV has yet to address itself to the very basic issues it should be concerned with. It is obvious that we need training of a different sort, a training that effects a merger of the academic and the producer, as we need, in this case, neither the pure academic nor the pure producer but an academic-producer or a producer-academic. What kind of training will it be? Who will give it? And who will be the clientele? These are the questions which need to be answered to take the very first steps towards making educational TV a reality.

2. It is believed that Doordarshan is already giving a lot of telecast time to educational programmes prepared at Educational Media Research Centres (EMRCs), arranged through UGC and other agencies, centrally as well as from the States.

In this connection, some commonplace observations are in order here:

> Very many schools have been given TV sets, presumably to be used for students. However, invariably these sets adorn the rooms of the principals and in many cases they are out of order and cannot be used.
>
> Most of these programmes are telecast twice a day, when all the learners concerned are at school/college/university. One wonders whether the programmes are really for the learners. Or are they for the general public, the masses!
>
> Besides, these programmes are mostly in English and therefore, they may not be serving even as educative TV.

Obviously, the problem is that of TV time. The prime time is allotted to news, current affairs, entertainment or popular serials—educational programmes have no place there. In such a situation, there is a strong case for a separate educational channel on which the entire time will be that of the learner. Will autonomous

Doordarshan have the institutional will and also the necessary funding available to create such a channel? If the funds are not available, will Doordarshan ignore this need!

3. Coming to the nature of educational TV, there is a major controversy regarding the programme—ordinary TV or fancy TV.

Ordinary TV may be the label given to any educational TV programmes used as mere extensions of the classroom. Perhaps a very good example of this kind of educational TV is available at Ramkhamhaeng University, Thailand, where one teacher/lecturer is projected through TV to hundreds of students seated in big halls. Such TV programmes are also used to bring an outstanding teacher, a well-known academic and the like alive to students thousands of miles away from the teacher/academic. Such educational TV saves time and money and yet provides enlightening educational exposure to learners.

Fancy TV, on the other hand, tries to be highly selective in each and every respect. The basic philosophy being that the educational potential rather than the extended reach of TV should be the basis for providing educational experiences through TV. In such programmes; television technology itself becomes the medium of instruction. For example, a learner can observe in great detail the life and activities of sub-marine plants and animal with the help of TV technology. Such exposure is not possible even in the best of classrooms otherwise. TV programmes of this type would obviously take a lot of time and money to produce, but they undoubtedly cover all the three domains that education is concerned with—Cognitive, Psycho-motor, and Affective.

Autonomous Doordarshan will have to take a stand in the controversy that rages between the two schools of thought—the one for ordinary TV and the other for fancy TV. It may be that the educational TV of autonomous Doordarshan works on a range between the ordinary and the fancy TV (for both have their strengths); and choose either, or a mix thereof depending on the needs of learners. The obvious implication is that for going into educational TV, autonomous Doordarshan will have to be concerned with not only the technicalities of their production, but also their theoretical bases.

4. As far as the clientele groups are concerned, educational TV will

have to cater to the needs of age-groups 5-14, 14-20/21 and above. In other words, care has to be taken not only of pedagogy but also that of andragogy. Looked at differently, the clientele groups consist of women, people living in remote areas, poor sections of the society, institutional labour and others. The obvious implication is that not only the academic relevance of the programmes but also the social relevance will have to be taken care of. In terms of the former, the issues involved are that of curriculum, themes and sub-themes within the curriculum, presentation of programmes, evaluation of programmes and the subsequent modifications of programmes. As for the issues of social relevance, a strong suggestion emerges that there also need to be programmes of a general nature. As of today none of these concerns forms the agenda for Doordarshan; autonomous Doordarshan will have to have an agenda of the type suggested above. Though Doordarshan has units responsible for education, in all probability they do not have the required level of professional know-how so essential to meet the demands outlined in the above paragraphs.

5. Lastly, we come to the issue of 'sharing the responsibility'. The present scenario is that in our country private sector has not shown any interest in educational TV so far and is not likely to do so for quite some time in the future as educational enterprise does not promise adequate returns—neither politically nor economically.

As far as the public sector is concerned, it is mainly the Central Government that has initiated activities like EMRCs, etc., to promote educational television. The problem which the public sector faces is partly born of its dependence on state directives (however covert they might be), and partly because of the absence of appropriate professionalism for educational TV. In the area of production, a major concern of the public sector seems to be the technical aspects of a programme. In order to produce a technically standard programme the public sector is inclined to depend on technicians more than academics. Secondly, the TV enterprise in the country being relatively new and also second hand technology (in the sense, we lag behind the Western World and whatever innovations we bring in are passed on to us by others), we have had no time in developing that kind of professionalism which synthesises production excellence with academic credibility. It must take us some time before we can claim our authority in this area.

Autonomous Doordarshan will do a great service to the country by working for that synthesis. Such synthesis should help TV become truly educational. A truly educational TV should attract the attention of the private sector too. This, I believe, is not wishful thinking, for there is evidence of such a phenomenon existing in the UK, the USA and Germany.

Let us go back to where we started. We said that today, except a few stray cases, there is hardly any educational TV in India. And then, hoping that autonomous Doordarshan will rise to the occasion, we set an agenda for it—an agenda consisting of five points. This five-point agenda is not comprehensive, it is not meant to be, but as an initial step. It sets goals and suggests a few ways to achieve some of them. We hope, autonomous Doordarshan will not be found wanting.

ANNEXURE I

Mass Media and Development*

Vikram Sarabhai

IN any developing country, one of the prime ingredients of development is the dissemination of information: information about new fertilizers, seeds, insecticides, cropping patterns, new technology, new findings and discoveries in all fields, new goods and services, new living patterns, etc. The process of education is basically related to an information dissemination/transfer process. For the rapid and sustained growth of developing countries, the urgent need to disseminate information to the masses is obvious.

Mass media are clearly the main components in this system of information transfer. Newspapers, movies, radio and television are the primary mass media. In India, we have a very large film industry—one of the biggest in the world. However, movie theatres are concentrated mostly in the larger towns and cities. Though there are some "travelling cinemas," which go around smaller towns and villages, these are few and a very small percentage of the total population is actually reached by them. Just over 4000 cinema theatres with a seating capacity of under three million are obviously inadequate for a population of over 500 million.

With the availability of inexpensive transistorised radio sets costing less than Rs. 100, the radio is becoming the medium with the largest coverage amongst the masses. The battery operated transistorised set has also permitted it to reach the population living in large number of unelectrified villages.

Television is ideal as a medium to convey information and news to the broad masses of people—particularly to the illiterate segment

* Originally presented at a conference of the Society for International Development in New Delhi, November 14-19, 1969.

of the population, on whom such an audio-visual medium would have a profound impact.

The following questions immediately arise in developing a television system for India.

(a) Should one concentrate on providing the benefits first to urban communities and progressively go to rural areas? Direct broadcast of TV from a satellite represents the use of an advanced technology, which for the first time does not impose a penalty on account of the dispersal of the receiving units away from urban centres. The Indian economy in the next two or three decades must lean heavily on the development of rural areas. It, therefore, seems to me urgently necessary to take effective steps to enrich life in the isolated rural communities. Moreover, for continued stability and national integration, following the division of the country into linguistic administrative units, there is need to bring together different units through a common mass media of communication reaching all sections of the population, the young and the old, men and women, the literate and the illiterate, the privileged and the under-privileged. I would submit, therefore, that the answer to this question can be clearly stated. It is that we should consciously reach the most difficult and least developed areas of the country and, because they are in this state, we should reach them in a hurry.

(b) In a state of economic and social backwardness, do we need to deploy imaginatively the most powerful techniques at our disposal or can we get by with less effective means? In concrete terms, can radio be an alternative to television? I suggest that television has a unique contribution to make, because, it has a rare credibility and is most persuasive.

(c) Can we regard TV largely as an instrument for development, an investment rather than an overhead of society? The answer to this question depends clearly on how we use the medium and who uses it. I cannot help noting that much depends on the objectives and the assumptions of those, who create the operating system. This is because the living culture of the system is determined by the people who are associated with it. I have no quarrel with those who wish to provide entertainment through media of mass communication for society, certainly needs entertainment. But, I cannot see the same people determining policies and programming content related to education of instruction through the same medium.

(d) Recognising that Government has a number of different

agencies responsible for individual fields such as information and broadcasting, education, agriculture, health, family planning, etc., how can one provide effective management of the system as a whole, along with use by the respective agencies of this powerful medium as an integral part of their promotional efforts? I would suggest that it should be possible for the other agencies to buy television time for programmes related to the discharge of their own responsibilities.

(e) Since Government has a very powerful role in promoting development, how can one prevent bureaucratisation of the system of mass communications with television? What could be the organisational framework in which programming initiative can be developed competitively amongst independent groups of innovative and imaginative producers and artists instead of through a monopolistic system, where just a few, official units produce all the programmes that are required? I would suggest that creation of a national authority, such as INTELSAT in the international scene, which merely owns, regulates and manages the mass communication system without itself taking total responsibility for software. Moreover, we should promote the development of agencies on a basis of redundancy to competitively provide software for individual clients who would buy time on the television system for promoting national objectives, which fall within subjects allocated to them. One would have to provide a feed-back system and an evaluation system to assist software development for developmental purposes.

It is quite clear that the problems of management and of software for television system to perform the role of an initiator of change and development are more formidable than the problem of hardware development. But, when we have worked through our problems and learnt through experience, we would have gained something far more precious from the standpoint of development than the television system.

ANNEXURE II

The Prasar Bharati Bill

(Speech of Shri P Upendra, Minister of Parliamentary Affairs and Information & Broadcasting, introducing the Bill in Lok Sabha)

MR Speaker, Sir, I rise to introduce in this august House the Prasar Bharati (Broadcasting Corporation of India) Bill, 1989. In doing so, I have the satisfaction of fulfilling a promise that the National Front had made to the people of the country. We had gone to the people with a manifesto containing a policy declaration to the effect that the National Front Government would liberate the electronic media from the control of the Government. The roots of this policy are to be found in the universal perception of the important role that Radio and Television play in the lives of our people and the influence that they have come to wield on the development and evolution of our society. Starting from humble beginnings, Radio programmes have today become available to almost 97 per cent of the population of our country and even Television, which started relatively recently, is now beaming its programmes to almost 76 per cent of our population. These two media have, therefore, become the prime sources for the dissemination of information and for providing education and entertainment to the people. In such a situation, it is essential to zealously guard the inalienable rights of our citizens to a free and unbiased flow of information and their right to be informed about what they wish to know and not only what others think that they should know. We believe, Sir, that no matter how enlightened the Government is, any control would, by definition, be an encroachment on this free flow of information and ideas. In a sense, therefore, the imposition of such control, represents the beginning of the destruction of a really free and democratic society to the ideals of which we are firmly committed.

We have, in the recent past, seen the brazen and uninhibited misuse of these two media for narrow, partisan purposes, resulting in the total destruction of their credibility, which is, and must always remain the most prized asset of any broadcasting system. There have been aberrations in the manner in which news and current affairs programmes with political and social content have been presented. The media have too often manipulated in total violation of the accepted norms. We had, in consequence, in keeping with our determination to bring in a fresh breeze of open comment, of a free flow of idea and information, promised to the people that we will not only stop such distortions and misuse, but, by law, free both the media from Governmental control. We have acted swiftly to end these distortions. I take pride in saying that even before the introduction of this Bill, we have taken decisive and energetic steps to free the broadcast media from day-to-day governmental control as regards newscasting and programming. The change is clearly discernible. The introduction of this Bill, Mr Speaker Sir, is a demonstration of our bonafides and our commitment to an ethos of true freedom and democracy.

Mr Speaker, Sir, I would like to draw your attention briefly to the background to the Bill which I am presenting today and to some of its salient features. The perception that electronic media can function unbiased only when they are autonomous, is not new. In our country, however, this perception has sharpened over the time, in keeping with the ever-increasing reach of Radio and Television. As far back as in 1964, the Government had appointed a committee under Shri A K Chanda which had examined the functioning of AIR, the only electronic medium broadcasting regularly at that time. This committee had observed and I quote:

> "It is not possible in the Indian context for a creative medium like broadcasting to flourish under a regimen(sic) of departmental rules and regulations. It is only by an institutional change that AIR can be liberated from the present rigid financial and administrative procedures of Government."

This committee had recommended the constitution of a separate corporation for Akashvani with freedom to evolve its own methods of recruitment, regulated scales of pay and conditions of service according to its needs and devise a financial and accounting system appropriate to its creative activities.

In 1977, following the trauma of the Emergency, one of the major objectives of the Janata Government was the granting of autonomy to AIR and Doordarshan. A committee had been appointed, under the Chairmanship of Shri B G Verghese, to examine the functioning of the two media and to make appropriate recommendations. On the basis of their recommendations, a Bill called the Prasar Bharati (Broadcasting Corporation of India) Bill was introduced in the Lok Sabha in 1979. This effort, however, came to naught as the Bill lapsed with the dissolution of the Lok Sabha.

Since then, with the expansion and new projects which have been implemented in the recent past, the influence that the two electronic media have come to wield, have assumed really gigantic proportions. The present Bill, therefore, although borrowing from the earlier one, also takes into account the changed circumstances and the present ethos.

In the present Bill, we are proposing, initially one Corporation be set up, with two wings one for Radio and other for Television. There will be a Board of Governors, with four full-time Governors, namely, Chairman, Executive Governor, Governor (Finance), and Governor (Personnel). In addition, there will be six part-time Governors who will be people of eminence in various fields of relevance to the two media. The two Directors-General of Radio and Television will report to the Executive Governor. We have provided for a method of appointment of the Chairman and Governors, which virtually does away with the Government's role in the process. They will be appointed by the President on the recommendations of a committee consisting of the Chairman of the Council of States, the Chairman of the Press Council and a nominee of the President of India. The independence of the Board of Governors has been further strengthened by providing that the Chairman and Governors, before the expiry of their terms, can only be removed in the same manner as prescribed for the removal of the Chairman and Members of the Union Public Service Commission in the Constitution.

Mr Speaker, Sir, you will notice that we have been at pains of define, in some detail, the objectives which will guide the Corporation in the discharge of its functions. This is necessary to ensure that the aspiration of the people of this country, belonging to diverse cultures, languages and regions, are fully met in the programming of these two media so that the variegated culture of the country is allowed to evolve, flourish and grow. We have also been conscious of the need for incorporating, within the structure of the Bill, a mechanism which will ensure that the functioning of the Corporation is never allowed to stray away from these objectives.

It is equally necessary to ensure that the rights and sensibilities of individuals and groups of people, which could be hurt by insensitive or biased programming, are not allowed to be infringed. It is in this context that a provision has been made for the establishment of a Broadcasting Council. This Council will examine all complaints of unfairness and bias or those relating to programmes not being in conformity with the objectives of the Corporation. This council will consist of a President who will function whole time. He will be assisted by ten other part-time Members, drawn from various walks of life, so that every aspect of programming could be brought under scrutiny. There is also a provision which will enable this Council to set up Regional Councils to cater to regional needs.

All senior appointments within the Corporation will be made by the Board of Governors and other appointments by recruitment boards to be set up by the Corporation under the rules. We have also provided Sir, protection to all categories of employees of AIR and Doordarshan, including officers of Indian Information Services working with these organisations. It will be our endeavour to ensure that all employees are treated justly and are provided opportunities and grow and develop in their own fields. I would, however, like to emphasize that the primary objective at all times would be to achieve excellence and there will be no place for persons who cannot contribute to it in a positive manner. Creativity and merit will have to be the final test. Necessary steps will be taken to ensure this.

The finances of the Corporation will be under-written by the Government on the touchstone of public service. Nevertheless, financial autonomy is to be promoted by providing that the Corporation shall have its own fund into which shall be paid broadcast receiver licence fees, if any advertisement revenue, service fees and other earnings. The External Broadcasting and Monitoring services shall be a charge on the government. The capital budget, likewise, will form part of plan expenditure. It is hoped that in due course Prasar Bharati will be financially viable and financial liability will become a realisable objective. A provision has been made to make the Corporation accountable to the Parliament.

Its Annual Report, incorporating a report by the Broadcasting Council will be placed before both Houses of Parliament to enable this august body to exercise scrutiny, debate over the manner in which the organisation has functioned and to give the required directions and guidances.

Sir, I am grateful to all the parties and their leaders, including the leader of the opposition, for their whole-hearted support to the Bill, the main features of which have been discussed with them as well as several experts, in informal discussions.

Sir, we are conscious that we need to move fast to bring the Corporation into being and yet not be hasty in proposing a structure which does not achieve our stated goals. It is in this context that during the next few months, before the Bill is actually taken up for consideration, we have planned to encourage different institutions and organisations to hold seminars, debates and discussions on all aspects of the proposed Corporation in addition to the panel discussions on the two media at various levels. It will be our endeavour to generate a national debate and to benefit from the many suggestions for improvements that will emanate as a result of this debate. We do not have any inhibition on this matter and will incorporate into the Bill such suggestions and ideas that further the aims and objectives that we have in mind. If the bill is taken up for consideration and passed around May 1990, it will still take time to draft the rules and regulations, appoint the governors, and other functionaries and place them in position. We shall endeavour to take the consequential steps following the passage of the Bill as expeditiously as possible. Even so, the appointed day may be about a year away. In the interregnum, Mr Speaker, Sir, it is not our intention to be idle or let things proceed as they are today. We are aware that much can be done immediately to ensure impartiality, objectivity and to give to the media the much-needed independence which will enable them to improve the quality of programmes. We intend, therefore, to undertake a comprehensive review of the programmes being broadcast and telecast by AIR and Doordarshan. We will examine all procedures and reconstitute the various committees and other bodies involved with programming, wherever necessary. New kinds of programmes will be considered. For example, we will try to increase the number of current affairs programmes and encourage independent producers to make them so that, fresh, thought-provoking ideas are placed before the audience. As regards Television, we will try to make the second channel in four metropolitan cities much more likely so that they can provide alternative programmes to meet the aspirations of the regional audiences.

To ensure that right from now all this is done through a process which is rooted in the concept of autonomy and independence, even before the law is enacted, we propose to immediately set up a compact five-Member Board, consisting of distinguished persons from the media, from the world of cinema, art and culture, the world of scholarship, agriculture and rural development, to oversee the functioning of AIR and Doordarshan. While it is true that this Board cannot at present, be given statutory powers, we will give it sufficient authority so as to enable it to ensure that programming is objective, impartial and of the highest quality. I propose to set up this Board very shortly, within the next few days.

Mr Speaker, Sir, the safeguards which have been built into this Bill with the objective of giving to the media the fullest protection from outside interference, both now and in the future, are as comprehensive as they can be. It must, however, be noted that ultimately it is the persons who direct and run the Corporation who will count. It is not only a structure that will bring the required independence, impartiality, objectivity, fairness and excellence. It is the people—the professionals who man the organisation—who will alone be able to do this. The structure will only enable them to bring these qualities to their work and protect them from the forces of various partisan interests. The responsibility which then devolves on those who work for the Corporation is indeed very large and onerous. The strictest vigilance will be needed to a process which is rooted in the concept of autonomy and independence, even before the law is enacted, we propose to immediately set up a compact five-Member Board, consisting of distinguished persons from the media, from the world or cinema, art and culture, the world of scholarship, agriculture and rural development, to oversee the functioning of AIR and Doordarshan. While it is true that this Board cannot at present, be given statutory powers, we will give it sufficient authority so as to enable it to ensure that programming is objective, impartial and of the highest quality. I propose to set up this Board very shortly, within the next few days.

Mr Speaker, Sir, the safeguards which have been built into

this Bill with the objective of giving to the media the fullest protection from outside interference, both now and in the future, are as comprehensive as they can be. It must, however, be noted that ultimately it is the persons who direct and run the Corporation who will count. It is not only a structure that will bring the required independence, impartiality, objectivity, fairness and excellence. It is the people—the professionals who man the organisation—who will alone be able to do this. The structure will only enable them to bring these qualities to their work and protect them from the forces of various partisan interests. The responsibility which then devolves on those who work for the Corporation is indeed very large and onerous. The strictest vigilance will be needed to eliminate corruption, arbitrariness and irresponsibility. The eyes of the entire nation will look to the Board of Governors to see how this goal is achieved. It will be our endeavour, as also the endeavour of my Ministry to provide all possible assistance.

Sir, the Bill I am introducing today is no ordinary Bill. It is a charter of freedom to give voice to the people of India, through the broadcast medium in fulfilment of their fundamental freedom of speech and expression as enshrined in Article 19 (I)A of the Constitution. This is a Bill for which the people have been waiting for long. I am sure it will be welcomed by all. The National Front has promised open government, dialogue, consensus and conciliation. This Bill is part of that promise. It is in this spirit that I take great pride and deem it a great privilege to introduce this historic Bill and commend it to this House and to the Nation.

With these words, Sir, I beg leave of the House to introduce the Prasar Bharati (Broadcasting Corporation of India)—1989.

ANNEXURE III

The Prasar Bharati (Broadcasting Corporation of India) Act, 1990

An Act

to provide for the establishment of a Broadcasting Corporation for India, to be known as Prasar Bharati, to define its composition, functions and powers and to provide for matters connected therewith or incidental thereto.

Chapter I

PRELIMINARY

Short title, extent and commencement.
1. (1) This Act may be called the Prasar Bharati (Broadcasting Corporation of india) Act, 1990. (2) It extends to the whole of India. (3) It shall come into force on such date as the Central Government may, by notification, appoint.

Definitions.
2. In this Act, unless the context otherwise requires,— (*a*) "Akashvani" means the offices, stations and other establishments, by whatever name called, which, immediately before the appointed day, formed part of or were under the Director-General, All India Radio of the Union Ministry of Information and Broadcasting; (*b*) "appointed day" means the date appointed under section 3; (*c*) "broadcasting" means the dissemination of any form of communication like signs, signals, writing, pictures, images and sounds of all kinds by transmission of electromagnetic waves through space or through cables intended to be received by the general public either directly or indirectly through the medium of relay stations and all its grammatical variations and cognate expressions shall be construed accordingly; (*d*) "Board" means the Prasar Bharati Board; (*e*) "Broadcasting Council" means the Council established under

The italics indicate amendments to the draft bill.

section 14; (*f*) "Chairman" means the Chairman of the Corporation appointed under section 4; (*g*) "Corporation" means the Prasar Bharati (Broadcasting Corporation of India) established under section 3; (*h*) "Doordarshan" means the offices, kendras and other establishments, by whatever name called, which, immediately before the appointed day, formed part of or were under the Directorate-General, Doordarshan of the Union Ministry of Information and Broadcasting; (*i*) *"elected Member" means a Member elected under section 3*; (*j*) "Executive Member" means the Executive Member appointed under section 4; (*k*) "kendra" means any telecasting centre with studios or transmitters or both and includes a relay station; (*l*) "Member" means a Member of the Board; (*m*) "Member (Finance)" means the Member (Finance) appointed under section 4; (*n*) "Member (Personnel)" means the Member (Personnel) appointed under section 4; (*o*) "Nominated Member" means the Member nominated by the Union Ministry of Information and Broadcasting under section 3; (*p*) "Non-lapsable Fund" means the Fund created from the commercial revenues of Akashvani and Doordarshan to meet expenditure on certain schemes; (*q*) "notification" means a notification published in the Official Gazette; (*r*) "Part-time Member" means a Part-time Member of the Board appointed under section 4, but does not include an *ex-officio* Member, the Nominated Member or an elected Member; (*s*) "prescribed" means prescribed by rules made under this Act; (*t*) "Recruitment Board" means a board established under sub-section (*1*) of section 10; (*u*) "regulations" means regulations made by the Corporation under this Act; (*v*) "station" means any broadcasting station with studios or transmitters or both and includes a relay station; (*w*) "Whole-Time Member" means the Executive Member, Member (Finance) or Member (Personnel); (*x*) "year" means the financial year.

Chapter II

PRASAR BHARATI
(BROADCASTING CORPORATION OF INDIA)

Establishment and composition of Corporation.

3. (1) With effect from such date as the Central Government may by notification appoint in this behalf, there shall be established for the purposes of this Act a Corporation, to be known as the Prasar Bharati (Broadcasting Corporation of India). (2) The Corporation shall be a body corporate by the name aforesaid, having perpetual succession and a common seal with power to acquire, hold and dispose of property, both movable and immovable, and to contract, and shall by the said name sue and be sued. (3) The headquarters of the Corporation shall be at New Delhi and the Corporation may establish offices, kendras or stations at other places in India and, with the previous approval of the Central Government, outside India. (4) The general superintendence, direction and management of the affairs of the Corporation shall vest in the Prasar Bharati Board which may exercise all such powers and do all such acts and things as may be exercised or done by the Corporation under this Act. (5) The Board shall consist of—(*a*) a Chairman; (*b*) one Executive Member; (*c*) one Member (Finance); (*d*) one Member (Personnel); (*e*) six Part-time Members; (*f*) *Director-General (Akashvani), ex-officio*; (*g*) *Director-General (Doordarshan), ex-officio*; (*h*) one representative of the Union Ministry of Information and Broadcasting, to be nominated by that Ministry; and (*i*) *two representatives of the employees of the Corporation, of whom one shall be elected by the engineering staff from amongst themselves and one shall be elected by the other employees from amongst themselves.* (6) The Corporation may appoint such committees as may be necessary for the efficient performance, exercise and discharge of its functions, powers and duties:

Provided that all or a majority of the members of each committee shall be Members and a member of any such committee who is not a Member shall have only the right to attend meetings of the committee and take part in the proceedings thereof, but shall not have the right to vote. (7) The Corporation may associate with itself, in such manner and for such purposes as may be provided by regulations, any person whose assistance or advice it may need in complying with any of the provisions of this Act and a person so associated shall have the right to take part in the discussions of the Board relevant to the purposes for which he has been associated, but shall not have the right to vote. (8) No act or proceeding of the Board or of any committee appointed by it under sub-section [6] shall be invalidated merely by reason of—(*a*) any vacancy in, or any defect in the constitution of, the Board or such committee; or (*b*) any defect in the appointment of a person acting as a Member or a member of such committee; or (*c*) any irregularity in the procedure of the Board or such committee not affecting the merits of the case.

Appointment of Chairman and other Members.

4. (1) The Chairman and the other Members, except the *ex-officio* Members, the Nominated Member and the elected Members shall be appointed by the President of India on the recommendation of a committee consisting of—(*a*) the Chairman of the Council of States, who shall be the Chairman of the Committee; (*b*) the Chairman of the Press Council of India established under section 4 of the Press Council Act, 1978; and (*c*) one nominee of the President of India. (2) No appointment of a Member shall be invalidated merely by reason of any vacancy in, or any defect in the constitution of, the committee appointed under sub-section [1]. (3) The Chairman and the Part-time Members shall be persons of eminence in public life; the Executive Member shall be a person having special knowledge or practical experience in respect of such matters as administration, management, broadcasting, education, literature, culture, arts, music, dramatics or journalism; the Member (Finance) shall be a person having special knowledge or practical experience in respect of financial matters and the Member (Personnel) shall be a person having special knowledge or practical experience in respect of personnel management and administration. (4) *The recommendations made by the committee constituted under sub-section [1] shall be binding for the purposes of appointments under this section.*

Powers and functions of Executive Member.

5. The Executive Member shall be the Chief Executive of the Corporation and shall, subject to the control and supervision of the Board, exercise such powers and discharge such functions of the Board as it may delegate to him.

Term of office, conditions of service, etc., of Chairman and other Members.

6. (1) The Chairman shall be Part-time Member and shall hold office for a term of six years from the date on which he enters upon his office. (2) The Executive Member, the Member (Finance) and the Member (Personnel) shall be Whole-time Members and very such Member shall hold office for a term of six years from the date

on which he enters upon his office or until he attains the age of sixty-two years, whichever is earlier. (3) The term of office of Part-time Members shall be six years, but one-third of such Members shall retire on the expiration of every second year. (4) *The term of office of an elected Member shall be two years or till he ceases to be an employee of the Corporation, whichever is earlier.* (5) As soon as may be after the establishment of the Corporation, the President of India may, by order, make such provision as he thinks fit for curtailing the term of office of some of the Part-time Members then appointed in order that one-third of the Members holding office as such Part-time Members shall retire in every second year thereafter. (6) Where before the expiry of the term of office of a person holding the office of Chairman, or any other Member, a vacancy arises, for any reason whatsoever, such vacancy shall be deemed to be a casual vacancy and the person appointed or elected to fill such vacancy shall hold office for the unexpired period of the term for which his predecessor in office would have held office if such vacancy had not arisen. (7) The Whole-time Members shall be the employees of the Corporation and as such shall be entitled to such salaries and allowances and shall be subject to such conditions of service in respect of leave, pension (if any), provident fund and other matters as may be prescribed:

Provided that the salaries and allowances and the conditions of service shall not be varied to their disadvantage after their appointment. (8) The Chairman and Part-time Members shall be entitled to such allowances as may be prescribed.

Removal and Suspension of Chairman and Members.

7. (1) Subject to the provisions of sub-section [3], the Chairman or any other Member, except an *ex-officio* Member, the Nominated Member and an elected Member shall only be removed from his office by order of the President of India on the ground of misbehaviour after the Supreme Court, on a reference being made to it by the President, has, on inquiry held in accordance with such procedure as the Supreme Court may by rules provide, reported that the Chairman or such other Member, as the case may be, ought, on such ground, be removed. (2) The President may suspend from office the Chairman or other Member, except an *ex-officio* Member, the Nominated Member or an elected Member, in respect of whom a reference has been made to the Supreme Court under sub-section

[1] until the President has passed orders on receipt of the report of the Supreme Court on such reference. (3) Notwithstanding anything contained in sub-section [1], the President may, by order, remove the Chairman or any Whole-time Member from his office if such Chairman or such Whole-time Member—(*a*) *ceases to be a citizen of India*; or (*b*) is adjudged an insolvent; or (*c*) engages during his term of office in any paid employment outside the duties of his office; or (*d*) is convinced of any offence involving moral turpitude; or (*e*) is, in the opinion of the President, unfit to continue in office by reason of infirmity of body or mind:

Provided that the President may, by order, remove any Part-time Member from his office if he is adjudged an insolvent *or is convicted of any offence involving moral turpitude* or where he is, in the opinion of the President, unfit to continue in office by reason of infirmity of body or mind. (4) If the Chairman or any Whole-time Member, except any *ex-officio* Member, the Nominated Member or any elected Member, is, or becomes in any way concerned or interested in any contract or agreement made by or on behalf of the Corporation or the Government of India or the Government of a State or, participates in any way in the profit thereof, or in any benefit or emolument arising therefrom than as a member, and in common with other members of an incorporated company, he shall, for the purposes of sub-section [1], be deemed to be guilty of misbehaviour. (5) If a Part-time Member is, or becomes in any way concerned, or interested in any contract, or agreement made by or on behalf of the Corporation, he shall, for the purposes of sub-section [1], be deemed to be guilty of misbehaviour. (6) The Chairman or any other Member may resign his office by giving notice thereof in writing to the President of India and on such resignation being accepted, the Chairman or other Member shall be deemed to have vacated his office.

Meetings of Board.

8. (1) The Board shall meet at such times and places and shall observe such rules of procedure in regard to the transaction of business at its meetings (including the quorum at meetings) as may be provided by regulations:

Provided that there shall not be less than six meetings every year but three months shall not intervene between one meeting and the next meeting.

(2) A Member shall be deemed to have vacated his office if he absents himself for three consecutive meetings of the Board without the leave of the Chairman. (3) The Chairman shall preside at the meetings of the Board and if for any reason he is unable to attend any meeting, the Executive Member and in the absence of both, any other Member elected by the Members present at such meeting, shall preside at the meeting. (4) All questions which come up before any meeting of the Board shall be decided by a majority of the votes of the Members present and voting and, in the event of an equality of votes, the Chairman, or in his absence, the person presiding, shall have and exercise a second or casting vote.

Officers and other employees of Corporation.
9. (1) Subject to such control, restrictions and conditions as may be prescribed, the Corporation may appoint, after consultation with the Recruitment Board, *the Director-General (Akashvani), the Director-General (Doordarshan)* and such other officers and other employees as may be necessary. (2) The method of recruitment of such officers and employees and all other matters connected therewith and the conditions of service of such officers and other employees shall be such as may be provided by regulations.

Establishment of Recruitment Boards.
10. (1) The Corporation shall, as soon as may be, after the appointed day and in such manner and subject to such conditions and restrictions as may be prescribed, establish for the purpose of section 9, one or more Recruitment Boards consisting wholly of persons other than the Members, officers and other employees of the Corporation:

Provided that for the purposes of appointment to the posts carrying scales of pay which are not less than that of a Joint Secretary to the Central Government, the Recruitment Board shall consist of the Chairman, other Members, *the ex-officio Members*, the Nominated Member and the elected Members. (2) The qualifications and other conditions of service of the members constituting the Recruitment Board and the period for which such members shall hold office, shall be such as may be prescribed.

Transfer of service of existing employees to Corporation.
11. (1) Where the Central Government has ceased to perform any

functions which under section 12 are the functions of the Corporation, it shall be lawful for the Central Government to transfer, by order and with effect from such date or dates as may be specified in the order, to the Corporation any of the officers or other employees serving in the Akashvani or Doordarshan and engaged in the performance of those functions:

Provided that no order under this sub-section shall be made in relation to any officer or other employee in the Akashvani or Doordarshan who has, in respect of the proposal of the Central Government to transfer such officer or other employee to the Corporation, intimated within such time as may be specified in this behalf by the Central Government, his intention of not becoming an employee of the Corporation.

(2) The provisions of sub-section [1] shall also apply to the members of the Indian Information Service, the Central Secretariat Service or any other service or to persons borne on cadres outside Akashvani and Doordarshan who have been working in Akashvani or Doordarshan immediately before the appointed day:

Provided that where any such member intimates, within the time specified in sub-section [1], his intention of not becoming an employee to the Corporation but to continue on deputation, he may be allowed to continue on deputation in accordance with such terms and conditions as may be prescribed.

(3) In making an order under sub-section [1], the Central Government shall, as far as may be, take into consideration the functions which the Akashvani or, as the case may be, Doordarshan has ceased or ceases to perform and the area in which such functions have been or are performed. (4) An officer or other employee transferred by an order under sub-section [1] shall, on and from the date of transfer, cease to be an employee of the Central Government and become an employee of the Corporation with such designation as the Corporation may determine and shall, subject to the provisions of sub-sections [5] and [6], be governed by such regulations as may be made as respects remuneration and other conditions of service including pension, leave and provident fund and shall continue to be an officer or other employee of the Corporation unless and until his employment is terminated by the Corporation.

(5) Every Officer or other employee transferred by an order made under sub-section [1] shall, within six months from the date of transfer, exercise his option, in writing, to be governed—(*a*) by the

scale of pay applicable to the post held by him in the Akashvani or Doordarshan immediately before the date of transfer or by the scale applicable to the post under the Corporation to which he is transferred; (*b*) by the leave, provident fund, retirement or other terminal benefits admissible to employees of the Central Government in accordance with the rules or orders of the Central Government, as amended from time to time, or the leave, provident fund or other terminal benefits admissible to the employees of the Corporation under the regulations, and such option once exercised under this Act shall be final:

Provided that the option exercised under clause [a] by an officer or other employee shall be applicable only in respect of the post under the Corporation to which such officer or other employee is transferred and on appointment to a higher post under the Corporation he shall be eligible only for the scale of pay applicable to such higher post:

Provided further that if immediately before the date of his transfer any such officer or other employee is officiating in a higher post under the Government either in a leave vacancy or any other vacancy of a specified duration, his pay on transfer shall be protected for the unexpired period of such vacancy and thereafter he shall be entitled to the scale of pay applicable to the post under the Government to which he would have reverted or to the scale of pay applicable to the post under the Corporation to which he is transferred, whichever he may opt:

Provided also that when an officer or other employee serving in the Union Ministry of Information and Broadcasting or in any of its attached or subordinate offices is promoted to officiate in a higher post in the Ministry or office subsequent to the transfer to the Corporation of any other officer or employee senior to him in that Ministry or office before such transfer, the officer or other employee who is promoted to officiate in such higher post shall, on transfer to the Corporation, be entitled only to the scale of pay applicable to the post he would have held but for such promotion or the scale of pay applicable to the post under the Corporation to which he is transferred, whichever he may opt.

(6) No officer or other employee transferred by an order made under sub-section [1] or sub-section [2],—(*a*) shall be dismissed or removed by an authority subordinate to that competent to make a similar or equivalent appointment under the Corporation as may be

specified in the regulations; (*b*) shall be dismissed or removed or reduced in rank except after an inquiry in which he has been informed of the charges against him and given a reasonable opportunity of being heard in respect of those charges:

Provided that where it is proposed after such inquiry to impose upon him any such penalty, such penalty may be imposed on the basis of evidence adduced during such inquiry and it shall not be necessary to give such person an opportunity of making representation on the proposed penalty:

Provided further that clause [b] shall not apply where an officer or other employee is dismissed or removed or reduced in rank on the ground of conduct which has led to his conviction on a criminal charge.

Functions and Powers of Corporation.

12. (1) Subject to the provisions of this Act, it shall be the primary duty of the Corporation to organise and conduct public broadcasting service to inform, educate and entertain the public and to ensure a balanced development of broadcasting on radio and television.

Explanation—*For the removal of doubts, it is hereby declared that the provisions of this section shall be in addition to, and not in derogation of, the provisions of the Indian Telegraph Act, 1885.*

(2) The Corporation shall, in the discharge of its functions, be guided by the following objectives, namely:—(*a*) upholding the unity and integrity of the country and the values enshrined in the Constitution; (*b*) safeguarding the citizen's right to be informed freely, truthfully and objectively on all matters of public interest, national or international, and presenting a fair and balanced flow of information including contrasting views without advocating any opinion or ideology of its own; (*c*) paying special attention to the fields of education and spread of literacy, agriculture, rural development, environment, health and family welfare and science and technology; (*d*) providing adequate coverage to the diverse cultures and languages of the various regions of the country by broadcasting appropriate programmes; (*e*) providing adequate coverage to sports and games so as to encourage healthy competition and the spirit of sportsmanship; (*f*) providing appropriate programmes keeping in view the special needs of the youth; (*g*) informing and stimulating the national consciousness in regard to the status and problems of women and paying special

attention to the upliftment of women; (*h*) promoting social justice and combating exploitation, inequality and such evils as untouchability and advancing the welfare of the weaker sections of the society; (*i*) safeguarding the rights of the working classes and advancing their welfare; (*j*) serving the rural and weaker sections of the people and those residing in border regions, backward or remote areas; (*k*) providing suitable programmes keeping in view the special needs of the minorities and tribal communities; (*l*) taking special steps to protect the interests of children, the blind, the aged, the handicapped and other vulnerable sections of the people; (*m*) promoting national integration by broadcasting in a manner that facilitates communication in the languages in India; and facilitating the distribution of regional broadcasting services in every State in the languages of that State; (*n*) providing comprehensive broadcast coverage through the choice of appropriate technology and the best utilisation of the broadcast frequencies available and ensuring high quality reception; (*o*) promoting research and development activities in order to ensure that radio and television broadcast technology are constantly updated; and (*p*) expanding broadcasting facilities by establishing additional channels of transmission at various levels.

(3) in particular, and without prejudice to the generality of the foregoing provisions, the Corporation may take such steps as it thinks fit—(*a*) to ensure that broadcasting is conducted as a public service to provide and produce programmes; (*b*) to establish a system for the gathering of news for radio and television; (*c*) to negotiate for purchase of, or otherwise acquire, programmes and rights or privileges in respect of sports and other events, films, serials, occasions, meetings, functions or incidents of public interest, for broadcasting and to establish procedures for the allocation of such programmes, rights or privileges to the services; (*d*) to establish and maintain a library or libraries of radio, television and other materials; (*e*) to conduct or commission, from time to time, programmes, audience research, market or technical service, which may be released to such persons and in such manner and subject to such terms and conditions as the Corporation may think fit; (*f*) to provide such other services as may be specified by regulations.

(4) Nothing in sub-sections [2] and [3] shall prevent the Corporation from managing on behalf of the Central Government and in accordance with such terms and conditions as may be specified by that Government the broadcasting of External Services and

monitoring of broadcasts made by organisations outside India on the basis of arrangements made for reimbursement of expenses by the Central Government. (5) *For the purposes of ensuring that adequate time is made available for the promotion of the objectives set out in this section, the Central Government shall have the power to determine the maximum limit of broadcast time in respect of the advertisement.* (6) The Corporation shall be subject to no civil liability on the ground merely that it failed to comply with any of the provisions of this section. (7) The Corporation shall have power to determine and levy fees and other service charges for or in respect of the advertisements and such programmes as may be specified by regulations:

Provided that the fees and other service charges levied and collected under this sub-section shall not exceed such limits as may be determined by the Central Government, from time to time.

Parliamentary Committee.

13. (1) *There shall be constituted a Committee consisting of twenty-two Members of Parliament, of whom fifteen from the House of the People to be elected by the Members thereof and seven from the Council of States to be elected by the Members thereof in accordance with the system of proportional representation by means of the single transferable vote, to oversee that the Corporation discharges its functions in accordance with the provisions of this Act and, in particular, the objectives set out in section 12 and submit a report thereon to Parliament.* (2) *The Committee shall function in accordance with such rules as may be made by the Speaker of the House of the People.*

Establishment of Broadcasting Council, term of office and removal, etc., of members thereof.

14. (1) There shall be established, by notification, as soon as may be after the appointed day, a Council, to be known as the Broadcasting Council, to receive and consider complaints referred to in section 15 and to advise the Corporation in the discharge of its functions in accordance with the objectives set out in section 12. (2) The Broadcasting Council shall consist of—(*i*) a President and ten other members to be appointed by the President of India from amongst persons of eminence in public life; (*ii*) *four Members of Parliament, of whom two from the House of the People to be nominated by the*

Speaker thereof and two from the Council of States to be nominated by the Chairman thereof. (3) The President of the Broadcasting Council shall be a whole-time member and every other member shall be a part-time member and the President or the part-time member shall hold office as such for a term of three years from the date on which he enters upon his office. (4) The Broadcasting Council may constitute such number of Regional Councils as it may deem necessary to aid and assist the Council in the discharge of its functions. (5) The President of the Broadcasting Council shall be entitled to such salary and allowances and shall be subject to such conditions of service in respect of leave, pension (if any), provident fund and other matters as may be prescribed.

Provided that the salary and allowances and the conditions of service shall not be varied to the disadvantage of the President of the Broadcasting Council after his appointment.

(6) The other members of the Broadcasting Council and the members of the Regional Council constituted under sub-section [4] shall be entitled to such allowances as may be prescribed.

Jurisdiction of, and the procedure to be followed by, Broadcasting Council.

15. (1) The Broadcasting Council shall receive and consider complaints from—(*i*) any person or group of persons alleging that a certain programme or broadcast or the functioning of the Corporation in specific cases or in general is not in accordance with the objectives for which the Corporation is established; (*ii*) any person (other than an officer or employee of the Corporation) claiming himself to have been treated unjustly or unfairly in any manner (including unwarranted invasion of privacy, misrepresentation, distortion or lack of objectivity) in connection with any programme broadcast by the Corporation. (2) A complaint under sub-section [1] shall be made in such manner and within such period as may be specified by regulations. (3) The Broadcasting Council shall follow such procedure as it thinks fit for the disposal of complaints received by it. (4) If the complaint is found to be justified either wholly or in part, the Broadcasting Council shall advise the Executive Member to take appropriate action. (5) If the Executive Member is unable to accept the recommendation of the Broadcasting Council, he shall place such recommendation before the Board for its decision thereon. (6) If the Board is also unable to accept the recommendation of the Broadcasting Council, it shall record its reasons therefor and inform the Broadcasting Council accordingly. (7) *Notwithstanding anything contained in sub-sections [5] and [6], where the Broadcasting Council deems it appropriate, it may, for reasons to be recorded in writing, require the Corporation to broadcast its recommendations with respect to a complaint in such manner as the Council may deem fit.*

Chapter III

ASSETS, FINANCES AND ACCOUNTS

Transfer of certain assets, liabilities, etc., of Central Government to Corporation.

16. As from the appointed day,—(*a*) all property and assets (including the Non-lapsable Fund) which immediately before that day vested in the Central Government for the purpose of Akashvani or Doordarshan or both shall stand transferred to the Corporation on such terms and conditions as may be determined by the Central Government and the book value of all such property and assets shall be treated as the capital provided by the Central Government to the Corporation; (*b*) all debts, obligations and liabilities incurred, all contracts entered into and all matters and things engaged to be done by, with or for the Central Government immediately before such day for or in connection with the purposes of Akashvani or Doordarshan or both shall be deemed to have been incurred, entered into and engaged to be done by, with or for the Corporation; (*c*) all sums of money due to the Central Government in relation to the Akashvani or Doordarshan or both immediately before such day shall be deemed to be due to the Corporation; (*d*) all suits and other legal proceedings instituted or which could have been instituted by or against the Central Government immediately before such day for any matter in relation to the Akashvani or Doordarshan or both may be continued or instituted by or against the Corporation.

Grants, etc., by Central Government.

17. For the purposes of enabling the Corporation to discharge its functions efficiently under this Act, the Central Government may,

after due appropriation made by Parliament by law in this behalf, pay to the Corporation in each financial year,— (*i*) the proceeds of the broadcast receiver licence fees, if any, as reduced by the collection charges; and (*ii*) such other sums of money as that Government considers necessary, by way of equity, grant-in-aid or loan.

Fund of Corporation.

18. (1) The Corporation shall have its own Fund and all the receipts of the Corporation (including the amounts which stand transferred to the Corporation under section 16) shall be credited to the Fund and all payments by the Corporation shall be made therefrom. (2) All moneys belonging to the Fund shall be deposited in one or more nationalised banks in such manner as the Corporation may decide. (3) The Corporation may spend such sums as it thinks fit for performing its functions under this Act and such sums shall be treated as expenditure payable out of the Fund of the Corporation.

Explanation—For the purposes of this section, "nationalised bank" means a corresponding new bank specified in the First Schedule to the Banking Companies (Acquisition and Transfer of Undertakings) Act, 1970 or a corresponding new bank specified in the First Schedule to the Banking Companies (Acquisition and Transfer of Undertakings) Act, 1980.

Investment of Moneys.

19. The Corporation may invest its moneys in the securities of the Central Government or any State Government or in such other manner as may be prescribed.

Annual Financial Statement of the Corporation.

20. (1) The Corporation shall prepare, in each financial year, an Annual Financial Statement for the next financial year showing separately—(*a*) the expenditure which is proposed to be met from the internal resources of the Corporation; and (*b*) the sums required from the Central Government to meet other expenses, and distinguishing—(*i*) revenue expenditure from other expenditure; and (ii) non-plan expenditure from plan expenditure.

(2) *The Annual Financial Statement shall be prepared in such form and forwarded at such time to the Central Government for its approval as may be agreed to by that Government and the Corporation.*

Accounts and Audit of Corporation.

21. (1) The Corporation shall maintain the proper accounts and other relevant records and prepare an annual statement of accounts in such form and in such manner as may be prescribed. (2) The accounts of the Corporation shall be audited by the Comptroller and Auditor-General of India and such intervals as may be specified by him and any expenditure incurred in connection with such audit shall be payable by the Corporation to the Comptroller and Auditor-General. (3) The Comptroller and Auditor-General and any person appointed by him in connection with the audit of the accounts of the Corporation shall have the same rights and privileges and authority in connection with such audit as the Comptroller and Auditor-General has in connection with the audit of Government accounts and, in particular, shall have the right to demand the production of books, accounts, connected vouchers and other documents and papers and to inspect any of the offices of the Corporation. (4) The accounts of the Corporation as certified by the Comptroller and Auditor-General of India or any other person appointed by him in this behalf together with the audit report thereon shall be forwarded annually to the Central Government and that Government shall cause the same to be laid before each House of Parliament.

Corporation not Liable to be Taxed.

22. Notwithstanding anything contained in the Income-tax Act, 1961, or any other enactment for the time being in force relating to income-tax or any other tax on income, profits or gains, the Corporation shall not be liable to pay any income-tax or any other tax in respect of—(*a*) any income, profits or gains, accruing or arising out of the Fund of the Corporation or any amount received in that Fund; and (*b*) any income, profits or gains, derived or any amount received, by the Corporation.

Chapter IV

MISCELLANEOUS

Power of Central Government to give directions.

23. (1) The Central Government may, from time to time as and when occasion arises, issue to the Corporation such directions as it may think necessary in the interests of *the sovereignty, unity and integrity of India* or the security of the State or preservation of public order requiring it not to make a broadcast on a matter specified in the direction or to make a broadcast on any matter of public importance specified in the direction. (2) Where the Corporation makes a broadcast in pursuance of the direction issued under sub-section [1], the fact that such broadcast has been made in pursuance of such direction may also be announced along with such broadcast, if the Corporation so desires. (3) A copy of every direction issued under sub-section [1] shall be laid before each House of Parliament.

Power of Central Government to Obtain Information.

24. *The Central Government may require the Corporation to furnish such information as that Government may consider necessary.*

Report to Parliament in certain matters and recommendations as to action against the Board.

25. (1) *Where the Board persistently makes default in complying with any directions issued under section 23 or fails to supply the information required under section 24, the Central Government may prepare a report thereof and lay it before each House of Parliament for any recommendation thereof as to any action (including supersession of the Board) which may be taken against the Board.* (2) *On the recommendation of the Parliament, the President may by notification supersede the Board for such period not exceeding six months, as may be specified in the notification:*

Provided that before issuing the notification under this sub-section, the President shall give a reasonable opportunity to the Board to show cause as to why it should not be superseded and shall consider the explanations and objections, if any, of the Board. (3) *Upon the publication of the notification under sub-section [2],*—(a) *all the Members shall, as from the date of supersession, vacate their offices as such*; (b) *all the powers, functions and duties which may, by or under the provisions of this Act be exercised or discharged by or on behalf of the Board, shall, until the Board is reconstituted under this Act, be exercised and discharged by such person or persons as the President may direct.* (4) *On the expiration of the period of supersession specified in the notification issued under sub-section [2], the President may reconstitute the Board by fresh appointments, and in such a case any person who had vacated his office under clause [a] of sub-section [3] shall not be disqualified for appointment:*

Provided that the President may, at any time before the expiration of the period of supersession, take action under this sub-section. (5) *The Central Government shall cause the notification issued under sub-section [2] and a full report of the action taken under this section to be laid before each House of Parliament.*

Office of member not to Disqualify a Member of Parliament.

26. It is hereby declared that the office of the member of the Broadcasting Council or of the Committee constituted under section 13 shall not disqualify its holder for being chosen as or for being a Member of either House of Parliament.

Chairman, Members, etc., to be public servants.

27. The Chairman and every other Member, every officer or other employee of the Corporation and every member of a Committee thereof, the President and every member of the Broadcasting Council or every member of a Regional Council or a Recruitment Board shall be deemed to be a public servant within the meaning of section 21 of the Indian Penal Code.

Protection of action taken in good faith.

28. No suit or other legal proceeding shall lie against the Corporation, the Chairman or any Member or officer or other employee thereof or the President or a member of the Broadcasting Council or a member of a Regional Council or a Recruitment Board for anything which is in good faith done or intended to be done in pursuance of this Act or of any rules or regulations made thereunder.

Authentication of Orders and other Instruments of Corporation.

29. All orders and decisions of the Corporation shall be authenticated by the signature of the Chairman or any other Member authorised by the Corporation in this behalf and all other instruments executed by the Corporation shall be authenticated by the signature of the Executive Member or by any officer of the Corporation authorised by him in this behalf.

Delegation of Powers.

30. The Corporation may, by general or special order, delegate to the Chairman or any other Member or to any officer of the Corporation, subject to such conditions and limitations, if any, as may be specified therein, such of its powers and duties under this Act as it may deem fit.

Annual Report.

31. (1) The Corporation shall prepare once in every calendar year, in such form and within such time as may be prescribed, an annual report giving a full account of its activities (including the recommendations and suggestions made by the Broadcasting Council and the action taken thereon) during the previous year and copies thereof shall be forwarded to the Central Government and that Government shall cause the same to be laid before each House of Parliament. (2) *The Broadcasting Council shall prepare once in every calendar year, in such form and within such time as may be prescribed, an annual report giving a full account of its activities during the previous year and copies thereof shall be forwarded to the Central Government and that Government shall cause the same to be laid before each House of Parliament.*

Power to make rules.

32. (1) The Central Government may, by notification, make rules for carrying out the provisions of this Act. (2) In particular, and without prejudice to generality of the foregoing power, such rules may provide for all or any of the following matters, namely:— (*a*) the salaries and allowances and conditions of service in respect of leave, pension (if any), provident fund and other matters in relation to the Whole-time Members under sub-section [7] of section 6; (*b*) the allowances payable to the Chairman and Part-time Members under sub-section [8] of section 6; (*c*) the control, restrictions and conditions subject to which the Corporation may appoint officers and other employees under sub-section [1] of section 9; (*d*) the manner in which and the conditions and restrictions subject to which a Recruitment Board may be established under sub-section [1] of section 10; (*e*) the qualifications and other conditions of service of the members of a Recruitment Board and their period of office under sub-section [2] of section 10; (*f*) the terms and conditions in accordance with which the deputation may be regulated under sub-section [2] of section 11; (*g*) the salary and allowances and conditions of service in respect of leave, pension (if any), provident fund and other matters in relation to the President of the Broadcasting Council under sub-section [5] of section 14; (*h*) the allowances payable to other members of the Broadcasting Council and the members of the Regional Councils, under sub-section [6] of section 14; (*i*) the manner in which the Corporation may invest its moneys under section 19; (*j*) the form and the manner in which the annual statement of accounts shall be prepared under sub-section [1] of section 21; (*k*) the form in which, and the time within which, the Corporation and the Broadcasting Council shall prepare their annual report under section 31; (*l*) any other matter which is required to be, or may be, prescribed.

Power to make regulations.

33. (1) The Corporation may, by notification, make regulations not inconsistent with this Act and the rules made thereunder for enabling it to perform its functions under this Act. (2) Without prejudice to the generality of the foregoing power such regulations may provide for all or/any of the following matters, namely—(*a*) the manner in which and the purposes for which the Corporation may associate with itself any person under sub-section [7] of section 3; (*b*) the times and places at which meetings of the Board shall be held and, the procedure to be followed threat, and the quorum necessary for the transaction of the business at a meeting of the Board under sub-section [1] of section 8; (*c*) the methods of recruitment and conditions of service of officers and other employees of the Corporation under sub-section [2] of section 9; (*d*) the remuneration and other conditions of service, including pension, leave and provident fund in relation to an officer or other employee of the Corporation under sub-section [4] of section 11; (*e*) the authority competent to make certain appointments referred to in clause [a] of sub-section [6] of section 11; (*f*) the services which may be provided by the Corporation under clause [f] of sub-section [3] of section 12; (*g*) the determination and levy of fees and other service charges in respect of advertisements and other programmes under sub-section [7] of section 12; (*h*) the manner in which and the period within which complaints may be made under sub-section [2] of section 15; (*i*) any other matter in respect of which provision is, in the opinion of the Corporation, necessary for the performance of its functions under this Act:

Provided that the regulations under [c] or clause [d] shall be made only with the prior approval of the Central Government.

Rules and Regulations to be laid before Parliament.

34. Every rule and every regulation made under this Act shall be laid, as soon as may be after it is made, before each House of Parliament, while it is in session for a total period of thirty days which may be comprised in one session or in two or more successive sessions, and if, before the expiry of the session immediately following the session or the successive sessions aforesaid, both Houses agree in making any modification in the rule or regulation, or both Houses agree that the rule or regulation should not be made, the rule or regulation shall thereafter have effect only in such modified form or be of no effect, as the case may be; so, however, that any such modification or annulment shall be without prejudice to the validity of anything previously done under that rule or regulation.

Power to remove difficulties.

35. If any difficulty arises in giving effect to provisions of this Act, the Central Government may, by order, published in the Official Gazette, make such provisions, not inconsistent with the provisions of this Act, as it may deem necessary, for the removal of the difficulty.

Provided that no such order shall be made after the expiry of a period of three years from the appointed day.

ANNEXURE IV

Radio and Television in Germany*

FOREIGNERS are often astounded at how many different radio stations there are in the federal Republic of Germany: there are over 30 public broadcasting station on the air, though not throughout the country. This variety is a consequence of the federal structure and of the fact that the Laender hold competence in the organization of broadcasting. This is why there are nine public broadcasting systems: Lower SAxony, Schleswig-Holstein and Hamburg have concluded an inner-state agreement on the Norddeutscher Rundfunk (North German Broadcasting) and the Laender: Rhineland-Palatinate and Baden-Wurttemberg have concluded one on the Sudwestfunk (Southwest Broadcasting). In Berlin (West), in addition to the Sender Freies Berlin (Free Berlin Broadcasting), there is also RIAS (Rundfunk im Amerikanischen Sektor / Broadcasting in the American Sector) run independently by the United States Information Service, though its president is German.

Central Broadcasting Stations

In 1960, two more broadcasting stations were founded to account for the interests of the Federal Republic of Germany as a whole. These are Deutsche Welle (The Voice of Germany) and Deutschlandfunk, both with headquarters in Colonge. Central government exercises a stronger influence on these two stations than on the broadcasting services of the Laender. Of the eleven members of the broadcasting council of Deutsche Welle two are elected from the Bundestag and two from the Bundesrat. Four are appointed by the government. At Deutschlandfunk, with a broadcasting council of 22 members, the Bundestag and the Bundesrat appoint six members each and the Government five members.

---

*Extracted from *Press and Broadcasting in the Federal Republic of Germany* by Georg Hellack, Inter Nationes, Bonn.

The task of Deutschlandfunk is to broadcast radio programmes for 'Germany and foreign countries in Europe'. The Government of the Federal Republic of Germany and the broadcasting services of the Laender participate in its financing whereas the federal government alone covers all the operating expenses for Deutsche Welle. In 1989, federal funds amounting to about 282,000,000 Marks were devoted to Deutsche Welle which broadcasts 93 programmes in German and 34 other languages on short wave every day. The major area of concentration is Africa, followed by southeast Europe, Asia, the Near and Middle East and finally Latin America. The amount of programming to North America is lower. This priority derives from the goal of Deutsche Welle to endeavour to redress the balance everywhere on earth where freedom of the press is lacking or restricted by censorship, i.e. where people are not given access to the sources of information in their own countries.

Foreign Stations

The stations operated by American, British and Canadian troops in the Federal Republic of Germany, primarily for soldiers and their families, are particularly popular with young people due to their music. In addition to these stations are two private American broadcasting station in Munich: Radio Free Europe and Radio Liberty which broadcast not for Germans but for the peoples of Eastern Europe under Communist rule.

A Common Roof

The nine broadcasting systems of the Laender, the two federal services and RIAS (in an advisory capacity) joined to form ARD, the '*Arbeitsgemeinschaft offentlich-rechtlicher Rundfunkanstalten der Bundesrepublik Deutschland*' (Network of the broadcasting Stations of the Federal Republic of Germany) to ensure public broadcasting, to bring about an internal financial balance, to facilitate an exchange of programmes, to run a common TV channel and to purchase films and series for all stations. The work of this common channel of ARD, German television channel 1, is coordinated by a programming conference.

The largest German Television Network

Though was already being given in the fifties to the foundation of a television company to compete with the television channel set up by

ARD which was criticised as being 'a TV monopoly' and politically one-sided. Initiatives came both from the federal government of the time under Konard Adenauer with the foundation of a German television company 'Deutschland-Fernsehen GmbH' and from federations of industry who had envisaged a private channel. On 28 February 1961, the Federal Constitutional Court banned government-owned television broadcasting as unconstitutional. It was then the turn of the prime ministers of the Laender who declared themselves willing to organise a second television channel. On the basis of the inner-state agreement of 6 June 1961, they founded ZDF, German television channel 2 with headquarters in Mainz as a corporation under public law. It is centrally operated in contrast to the broadcasting services of the Laender which were federally designed. Seats in the television council are held by representatives of the Laender, political parties at the federal level and representatives of the federal governmnt. In addition, as in ARD, major public organizations are also represented. ZDF operates one common channel for all of the Federal Republic of Germany with a budget of 1,627,000,000 Marks (1989), of which television fees represent 55 per cent.

Supervision and Control by the Public

A public form was chosen for broadcasting to ensure its independence from government and to enable the public to be represented ir the supervisory boards. Supervision and management of the public l roadcasting services are in the hands of three boards:

1. *Broadcasting Council*: Its members defend the interests of the public. They are either elected directly by the parliaments of the Laender or appointed directly by the political parties, religious communities, business and cultural organizations.
2. *Administrative Council*: Its members are elected by the Broadcasting Council. It ensures that broadcasting guidelines are respected, authorizes budget proposals and supervises management. It also elects the president who must be confirmed by the Broadcasting Council.
3. *Auxiliary Programming Council*: This council provides programming advice to the president. Its members elect the Broadcasting Council from candidates proposed by cutural, academic, business, youth, and sports organizations and

institutions, etc.

The president manages the station in accordance with the decision of the Broadcasting and Administrative Councils and is responsible for programming. Since the direct or indirect influence of political parties and groups of a Land makes itself felt in the composition of the Broadcasting Council which makes the main decisions, the station is occasionally criticized as being left-wing or right-wing according to whether the government of the Land is run by the Social-Democratics or Christian-Democratics.

Financing

The most important factor in the finances of the stations are the broadcasting fees, the level of which is set by the Prime Ministers of the Laender. At the present, the basic fee for radio is DM 5.16 and for television DM 11.44 such that households with registered radios and television sets pay a monthly broadcasting fee of DM 16.60. On 1 January 1990, the broadcasting fee is to be raised to a monthly DM 19.00. Two per cent of the broadcasting fee goes to the Laender to finance the activities of private broadcasting in general (technical infrastructure, open channels). The German Post Office also charges for satellite channels received by parabolic antennas and for the use of cable connections.

The broadcasting service of ARD receive 70 per cent of the television fees and ZDF 30 per cent. In 1988, a total of 3,640,000,000 Marks in fees were received by the broadcasting services of ARD, and a further 873,000,000 Marks in television fees went to ZDF.

Each broadcasting station is responsible for its own advertising. In 1988, the ARD stations had a total after-tax revenue of 1,622,000,000 Marks in advertising. ZDF made 632,000,000 Marks from the sale of broadcasting time in 1988.

The fees are collected centrally and distributed to the various stations according the number of listerners and viewers in the area in question. The proportions vary from 25.6 per cent for the *Westdeutscher Rundfunk* (West German Broadcasting) to 1.2 per cent for Radio Bremen. An internal financial adjustment also takes place, however, so that broadcasting services covering a small area can compete in programming. The German Post Office receives a constant percentage for technical services. It distributes frequencies and runs part of the broadcasting network.

Many Sources, One Channel

The broadcasting services of the Laender supply, in accordance with a specific ratio, their own productions to the common television channel broadcast by the stations of ARD. There are also joint productions such as centrally purchased feature films and series, contributions from Eurovision and programmes produced by one station on behalf of all the others. The most important are the news programmes 'Tagesschau' and 'Tagesthemen' prepared at the studios of the Norddeutscher Rundfunk (North German Broadcasting-NDR) in Hamburg.

The broadcasting hours of the ARD television channel have been substantially increased recently since some of the private channels operate twenty-four hours a day. Channels 1 and 2 have a joint morning programme; since autumn 1989 both stations have their own programmes from mid-day to the late night. Between 17:30 and 20:00 the ARD stations broadcast regional programmes with advertising of up to 20 minutes. There is no advertising later in the evening. Parallel to the programmes of Channel 1, there is also a third channel run by the various broadcasting stations, often with several stations using the same programmes. The programme structure is more or less as follows: almost 50 per cent of broadcasting time is devoted to information, and the other 50 per cent to games, music and entertainment.

ARD and ZDF broadcast further channels of cultural interest via satellite: ARD in co-operation with the Swiss Radio and Television Society have been broadcasting a channel called '1 Plus' since March 1986; ZDF has also been in co-operation with the Swiss Radio and Television Society and with the Austrian Broadcasting Company for '3-SAT' since December 1984. Negotiations on a joint Franco-German channel planned via satellite for 1991 in the two countries, in the success of which both governments are strongly interested, were bogged down for quite a while on the question of finance. The German portion of the costs amounting to an estimated 120,000,000 Marks is now to be covered by raising the broadcasting fees in 1993.

ARD and ZDF are working jointly with RAI in Italy, Antenna 2 in France and the BBC in Great Britain on a projected multilingual channel devoted exclusively to news broadcasts. Broadcasting is to begin in 1991 and is designed to counter similar plans of private broadcasting interests.

INDEX